T0319207

Critical Perspectives on the Theory and Practice of Translating Camfranglais Literature

Peter Wuteh Vakunta

Langaa Research & Publishing CIG
Mankon, Bamenda

Publisher
Langaa RPCIG
Langaa Research & Publishing Common Initiative Group
P.O. Box 902 Mankon
Bamenda
North West Region
Cameroon
Langaagrp@gmail.com
www.langaa-rpcig.net

Distributed in and outside N. America by African Books Collective
orders@africanbookscollective.com
www.africanbookscollective.com

ISBN: 9956-763-04-7

Dedication

For my forefathers
who perished translating orally for colonialists

Table of Contents

Acknowledgement

George Kubler(1962) observes that every artist works in the dark, guided only by the tunnels of earlier works. Accordingly, the creative process anticipates a knowledge that can be understood and articulated only a posteriori. In a similar vein, *Critical Perspectives on the Theory and Practice of Translating Camfranglais Literature* is the bye-product of sustained engagement with works by experts in the field of translation.

The inspiration to write this book stemmed from my teaching of works written in Camfranglais by literary scholars and socio-linguists, namely Jean-Paul Kouega (2013); André-Marie Ntsobé (2008); Hector Kamdem Foukoua(2015) Mercédès Fouda(2001); Patrice Nganang (2001) Edmond Biloa (2004, 2006) and Gabriel F. Kuitche (2001). I owe these genuine intellectuals a debt of gratitude. I owe a special debt of gratitude to my 'LANG 321: Introduction to Translation Studies' learners at the University of Indianapolis, United States of America, whose syllogistic discourses and pointed criticisms have served as a spring-board for the formulation of the premise of this book. For permission to translate excerpts from Mercédès Fouda's novella, *Je parle camerounais: pour un renouveau francofaune* (2001), I thank the writer and her publishers at Karthala in Paris-France.

Preface

Camfranglais fictional works are not canonical texts; rather they find a niche in the corpus of peripheral ethnographic texts that require an interpretive approach to literary discourse analysis and translational studies. In the light of the multilayered substratum from which Camfranglais literature derives its special qualities, it is incumbent on translators to have recourse to multidimensional frameworks in a bid to accomplish faithful translation—one such model, namely the *Hermeneutic-Exegetic model* is discussed in this book. We argue throughout this book that a serious exegetical study of the source text is the sine qua non of high quality translation (Magot, 1975); the moreso because the quintessence of translation is to produce a text that is faithful to the source text and in conformity with the structures of the target language. The purpose of translaton, after all, is to communicate to others what has been said or written in a foreign language (Vinay and Darbelnet, 1958). To paraphrase Margot again, the finality of translation is to transmit a message from a foreign language into the mother tongue of a particular group of readers who do not know the foreign langage in question. Thus, the translator must steer clear of subverting the exegetical process through skewed reading of the source text. The ramification of this injunction is that in addition to the exegetical endeavor, that is, the effort to understand the orginal text in its wider(literary, temporal, spatial, cultural, etc) context, the translator is expected to engage in a detailed unravelling of the universe of discourse in which the translation is intended to be utilized. This interpretative reading of the source text should take into account not just the linguistic elements of the source text but also the extra-linguistic factors that occasioned the conceptualization of the text in question. In the realm of translation studies, 'exegesis' stands for research into the background of an author, his woldview, influences exerted upon him by the milieu in which he or she lives and works as well as his or her creative genius. Interestingly, it is desirable for the exegete-translator to stand back from the details of the source text in a bid to internalize its functioning and general structure. A successful application of the *Hermeneutic-Exegetic* model discussed in this book requires that the translator must wrestle against some of the presumptions that confine the practice of translation to the mere replacement of linguistic material in one text with equivalent linguistic material in another text(Catford, 1965). This approach presupposes that words in other languages are endowed with the capacity to bear foreign concepts, or that an equivalent concept exists in another language (Papastergiadis, 2000). Translation, if executed faithfully, is seen as either retaining or reflecting back the original meaning. From this perspective, translation can be perceived as interpreting and transforming the source text in a bid to create an equivalence in the target language. It is in this vein that Walter Benjamin(1968) argues that the task of the translator is one which consists in finding that intended effect upon the language into which he or she is translating which produces in it the echo of the original. To put this differently, to translate is to transport meaning from one linguistic code to another; it involves taking cognizance of the equivalence as well as the intransigence implied in the translation process.

"Translation is the language of languages. It opens the gates of national and linguistic prisons. It is thus one of the most important allies of world literature and global consciousness."—**Ngugi wa Thiong'o,** *Globalectics* **(2012)**

Chapter One

Introduction

If up to a certain point, fiction writers have to re-invent language in a bid to appeal to a broader readership, the situation of Camfranglais writers is peculiar in that for them, French is not an acquisition; rather it is an occasion for constant mutation and modification. Engaged as they are, in the game of linguistic manipulation, these writers have to create their own language of fiction in a multilingual context affected by signs of polyglossia. To this end, Cameroonian Camfranglais creative writers constantly resort to code-switching as a mode of linguistic and cultural appropriation. Code-switching refers to the alternate use of more than one code in a single speech act, a phenomenon that Haugan refers to as "the alternate use of two languages, including everything from the introduction of a single unassimilated word up to a complete sentence or more into the context of another language" (cited in Omole, 58). In other words, Camfranglais writers tend to transpose the imprint of their cultural backgrounds onto fictional works, thereby creating a third code—Camfranglais. Camfranglais is a hybrid language spoken in the Republic of Cameroon where English, French and 248 indigenous languages co-exist. It is a medley of French, English, Pidgin and borrowings from local languages. Kouega (2003) defines Camfranglais as a "composite language consciously developed by secondary school pupils who have in common a number of linguistic codes, namely French, English and a few widespread indigenous languages."(23)

In a similar vein, Fonkoua (2015) observes that "Camfranglais is an outgrowth of codeswitching and codemixing patterns that have become fixed on emblematic lexical items."(13) He further notes that this phenomenon is particularly noticeable in places where there is significant contact between speakers of Pidgin English and speakers of (Cameroonian) French. In other words, the roots of Camfranglais are to be found in the language contact between inhabitants of towns in the former Southern Cameroons and those of the former French Cameroon. Mbah Onana holds that Camfranglais is *"une tentative de fabrication d'une langue de la rue intégrant tous les éléments des langues nationales occidentales, africaines, un peu à l'image de l'esperanto"* (cited in Zang Zang, 2014, p.9) [an attempt at fabricating a street language that integrates western national and African languages to produce a code that is, more or less, akin to Esperanto.]

Carole de Feral (1989: 20), on her part, posits that Camfranglais saw the light of day in the 1970s when youths in Douala indulged in a language practice she refers to as 'Français Makro'[1] Some examples of Camfranglais expressions that one is likely to hear in the streets in French-speaking Cameroonian cities such as Yaoundé, Douala, Bafoussam, Nkongsamba and more include:

> *Depuis le matin j'ai seulement chop une banane*= I have only eaten a banana since morning.
> *Gars je go damba*= I am going to play soccer, man.
> *Mon cochambrier a travel au day*= my room-mate has traveled today.
> *C'est moi qui comot avec la nga-ci*= I am going out with this girl.
> *La nkane-ci est trop coller chewing gum*=This girl has a gumshoe attitude.

---

[1] Makro is a popular Cameroonian derogatory word that means "thief" , "crook" or "rascal"(Fonkoua,2015)

Je suis dans le débé, je n'ai plus da do= I am in dire straits, I have no money left.

Je dois go regarder le saka= I have to go watch the dance.

La damer de la mater est très mo= Mom's food is very delicious.

Il a décalé avec mes do= He took off with my money.

Tu as nang où yesterday? =Where did you pass the night yesterday?

Tu vas go au sukul au day?=Are you going to school today?

A few more examples culled from Jean-Marie Ntsobé's book (2008) are quite revealing of the linguistic evolution that French has undergone in Cameroon:

All les gars du kwat-ci sont les ndosses= All the guys in this neighborhood are thieves.

Il y a le monde là-bas flop= There is a crowd over there.

Il y a one body qui est came te gnia ici= Somebody came looking for you here.

Buy-nous les arachides on tuyau= Buy us some peanuts to eat.

Le foup-foup que tu veux me bring-là ne doit pas waka avec moi= The confusion you're trying to cause will not work with me.

Le day ou tu vas me do ça n'est pas encore reach= The day on which you'll be able to do that to me is still far off.

It is noteworthy that the insertion of Camerounismes[2] such as "chop", "débé", "damba", "au day", "damer", "do", "sukul", "nga", "mo", "nkane", "saka", "commot", "flop", "kwat" and "foup-foup" in a French language text may obfuscate meaning for a translator unfamiliar with the significations embedded in these words that originate from Cameroonian indigenous languages and pidgin English. It is

---

[2] Cameroonian turns of phrase

3

obvious from these examples that the sentence structure of Camfranglais is calqued on the French syntactic structure, supported by loanwords from native tongues. Each utterance above contains at least one English, Pidgin or indigenous language word. This book addresses major translation challenges posed by language mixing. Rather than dwell on theories of translation, our approach is to bring new insights to the pragmatics of literary translation—ways in which the translator grapples with meaning discernment and rendition when faced with the task of translating texts couched in more than one language. Jacques Derrida (1985) reminds us in "Des Tours de Babel" of "one of the limits of theories of translation: all too often they treat the passing from one language to another and do not sufficiently consider the possibility for languages to be implicated *more than two* in a text. How is a text written in several languages at a time to be translated? How is the effect of plurality to be 'rendered'? And what of translating with several languages at a time, will that be called translating?"(171) The dilemma is no easier to solve for practicing translators. There are clear and obvious benefits of linguistic hybridity (i.e. a larger audience, self-representation, etc.) but how do these benefits transform when these languages are contextualized in literature? And what are the ramifications of such complicity or variance for the literary translator? What forms of discursive agencies are made available through translation? Critics of postcolonial literatures often contend that because of the quintessential hybridity of the postcolonial text, it is not possible for writers to return to an absolute pre-colonial cultural purity, nor is it possible for these writers to write fiction that is entirely independent of implication in the colonial discourse (Ashcroft et al., 1989; Bandia 1993; Eco, 2001; Gyasi, 2006; Jameson, 1986; Khatibi, 1983; Quayson, 2000; Riccardi, 2002; Robinson, 2012; Steiner,

4

1975; Tonkin and Frank,2010; Venuti, 1995). This remark is pertinent to the premise of our discourse in this book given the emphasis we place on linguistic hybrization in the creative writing process and the impact it may have on cross-cultural translation practice. Camfranglais writers tend to be perpetually adrift between several languages, vacillating from one culture to the other. Positioned on the threshold of 'adversarial' languages, Camfranglais literature opens up an in-between (third) space of linguistic ambivalence.in this vein, the writer becomes the bearer of a split consciousness and double vision. The question that begs the asking is how the translator comes to terms with this variance. This book attempts to provide answers to the foregoing intriguing interrogations. To this end, a corpus of four Cameroonian texts written in Camfrangalis has been selected for critical analysis— *Camfranglais* (2013) by Jean-Paul Kouega, *Temps de chien:chronique animale* (2001) by Patrice Nganang; *Moi taximan* (2001) by Gabriel Fonkou and *Je parle cameroonais: pour un renouveau francofaune* (2001) by Mercédès Fouda.The finality of the literary analysis we have embarked upon is to propose a canon that is deemed germane for the translation of Camfranglais fictional works written in an odd mix of codes as evidenced in the following chapter.

Chapter Two

Unpacking Code-Mixing in the Camfranglais Literary Text

In an attempt to transpose the imprint of their socio-cultural backgrounds into their fictional works; Camfranglophone writers make a deliberate attempt to indigenize standard French language through a process described by Zabus (1991) as "the writer's attempt at textualizing linguistic differentiation and at conveying African concepts, thought-patterns, and linguistic features through the ex-colonizer's language" (3) as seen in the following excerpt: *"Il y a la galère au Camer au day"* (Kouega 2013, p. 155) [There is harship in Cameroon nowadays][3]. It should be noted that the word 'Camer' is a truncation of the proper noun 'Cameroon'. In a similar vein, the expression 'au day' is a hybrid word derived from a combination of the first syllable of the French word 'aujourd'hui' and the second syllable of the English word 'today'. Thus, 'au day' is a neologism obtained by replacing the 'jourd'hui' segment of the word 'aujourd'hui' with the English word 'day.' 'Galère' is a French word that generically signifies 'hassle' or 'trouble.' However, in the speech of Camfranglones, this word has undergone a semantic shift and has taken on a new signification— 'hardship'. Semantic shifts such as this one is likely to make the job of the translator an uphill task, especially translators who are not familiar with the linguistic appropriation process that takes place in the art of creative writing in Cameroon as seen in the following statement: *"Ma friend se call Suzy, elle me help bad"* (Kouega, 154) [My friend's

---

[3] All translations are mine except otherwise indicated

7

name is Suzie; she helps me a lot]. It is interesting to note that the English adjective 'bad' carries a positive undertone in the speech pattern of speakers of Camfranglais. Thus, the phrase 'helep bad' could be rendered as 'helps me a lot.' This oxymoronic construction could be mistranslated literally as 'helps me badly" by an inattentive literary translator. Doing so would clearly derail the communicative intent of the fiction writer, an aspect of discourse analysis that André Lefevere (1992) describes as the author's "universe of discourse" (87). He further notes that on the universe-of-discourse level, translators may be faced with things, customs, and concepts that were immediately intelligible to the readers of the original but are no longer intelligible to prospective readers of the translation. It is noteworthy that the Pidgin English word 'helep' in the example above is derived from the Standard English word 'help.' It is evident from these examples that Camfranglais lexicon has been enriched abundantly by borrowings from Cameroon Pidgin English, also called Cameroonian Creole. Borrowings from Pidgin are evident in the following excerpt: *"Elle do the bayam-sellam depuis quand?"*(Kouega, 152). How long has she been doing bayam-sellam?] The compound word 'bayam-sellam' is derived from two Standard English words 'buy' and 'sell.' This neologism, the brainchild of Camfranglais speakers, is often used to describe a man or woman who retails foodstuff in the farmers' market. It goes without saying that retail trade has contributed significantly to the broadening of the lexicon of Camfranglais as seen in this example: *"J'ai des aff à placer"* [I have some items to sell] (Kouega, 122). More often than not, the task of the Camfranglais translator becomes onerous not only on account of loanwords from other languages such as "aff" and "do" as seen in the examples above but also on account of the fact that, very often, new semantic significations are appended to existing words. Notice that the word 'aff' is derived through the process of clipping. 'Aff' is a truncation of the French word 'affaires' which could literally be rendered as 'affairs' or 'business'. However, translating the word 'aff' literally would be tantamount to an under-translation because "aff" refers to 'stolen goods' in the Camfranglais universe of discourse.

Oftentimes, speakers of Camfranglais resort to code-mixing out of the desire to create humor as is noticea*ble* in the following statement: *"Il est tellement pressé qu'il a put son calékoum à l'envers* (Kouega, 154) [He is in such a hurry that he has worn his underwear inside out.]The word 'calékoum' is a *camerounisme*[4] for the French word *'caleçon'* [pant or underwear]. The code-switching in this statement is evident. We have the standard English word 'put', and the Pigin English word 'calékoum' jostling for space with standard French words. Omole (1998) maintains that this linguistic mixing presupposes a degree of proficiency at two or more languages from which a speaker or writer can switch back and forth seamlessly. These examples bear testimony to the fact that Camfranglais speakers tend to rely on code alternation as a word formative process as this other example seems to suggest: *"Ma rese a tcha le bele et elle talk que c'est avec un attaquant"*(Kouega, 129) [My sister is pregnant and she says that the man responsible is a taxi driver assistant]. Notice that the French word 'attaquant' is a standard French language word that could be translated literally as 'assailant' or 'attacker.' However, doing so would misrepresent the speaker's communicative intention because in this context the word *'attaquant'* has been endowed with an entirely new signification, 'taxi driver assistant.' Kouega defines the word 'bele' as "unwanted pregnancy" (138). The word 'tcha' is a Pidgin English word that could be rendered as "catch"; in this

---

[4] Cameroonian speech pattern

9

context catch a pregnancy as Cameroonians would have it. In other words, become pregnant. These examples lend credibility to the assertion according to which the task of the Camfranglais translator is not a sinecure, the more so because word-play has become the hallmark of Camfranglais speech pattern as the following statement suggests: *"Le djo-là est fini: sa nga a tcha le bele et elle veut qu'ils move ça et il n'a pas le do"* (Kouega, 138-9) [The boy over there is in trouble: his girlfriend is pregnant and she wants them to remove the foetus but he does not have any money.] Many borrowed lexical items are identifiable in this statement: 'djo' is culled from one of the vernacular languages spoken in Cameroon. It refers to 'man', friend' or 'partner.' 'Tcha' has other semantic equivalents: 'catch someone red-handed,' 'arrest someone,' 'hold,' and 'take someone along with force' (Kouega, 158). The word 'do' refers to 'money' as used in the following excerpt: *"Il m'a give les do que je lui ai ask hier* (Kouega, 181) [He gave me the money I asked for yesterday]. Notice that some words are spelled variably in Camfranglais. The word 'give', for instance, is sometimes written as 'gif', 'gib', 'gip', or 'gi' (Kouega, 197). This orthographical variation harbors bottlenecks for the unwary translator. Worse still, these heteronyms carry the germ of ambiguity for translators who have not mastered the rudiments of Camfranglais speech patterns. These examples lend credibility to the postulation according to which polysemy is part and parcel of Camfranglais discourse as the following example suggests: *Je suffer ici trop; better je go"* (Kouega, 140) [I suffer a lot here; I would rather leave]. It is interesting to note that the word 'better' collocates with the word 'suffer' that has a negative undertone as opposed to the signification of the same word in the following statement: *"J'étais un peu sick, mais ça va better"* (Kouega, 140) [I was a little sick but I am feeling better.]

It is important to underscore the fact that this mode of writing is not an indication of the fiction writer's inability to communicate using standard French. On the contrary, it is a deliberate quest for self-identification as ex-colonized writers endeavor to decolonize postcolonial literatures. As Ashcroft et al. (1989) would have it,

> What each of these literatures has in common beyond their special and distinctive regional characteristics is that they emerge in their present form out of the experience of colonization and the tension with the imperial power, and by emphasizing their differences from the assumptions of the imperial centre. It is this which makes them distinctively postcolonial. (2)

A critical reading of Kouega's text lends itself to the contention according to which the African palimpsest is at work in the creative writing process, a phenomenon described by Zabus (1991) as the African writer's "attempts to simulate the character of African speech in a Europhone text..." (101) Thus, the translator of Kouega's text is expected to uncover the cultural layers and contesting indigenous languages in ferment behind the apparently homogenous French language. To paraphrase Ashcroft et al. again (1989), language appropriation is deliberate and emerges in its present form "out of the experience of colonization and the tension with the imperial power... (2). In other words, the ex-colonized writer tends to turn the reality of colonial history on its head by writing back to the imperial center from the empire. This transpires when indigenous peoples begin to write their own histories using the ex-colonizer's language. Linguistic appropriation permeates all facets of Camfranglais fictional writing including the sex industry.

This industry has enriched the lexicon of Camfranglais speakers with a gamut of words that may have implications for faithful literary translation as seen in the following excerpt: *"J'ai tchouké la nga-là mais je n'ai pas bien hia moh"* (Kouega, 297) [I have screwed that girl but I did not enjoy it] (297). 'Tchouké' comes from the verbal infinitive 'tchouker' which could be translated literally as 'to fix in position using a wedge'. Rendering the sentence above as "I have fixed that girl in position using a wedge", or "I have put a wedge between that girl's legs" would be a blooper! The lexeme 'hia,' derives from the Standard English word 'hear.' In this context, it conveys the idea of 'have a feeling.' The contextual usage of these words may not be obvious to a translator unaccustomed to the semantic jugglery that is the hallmark of Camfranglais, thus amplifying the likelihood of undertranslation or outright mistranslation. 'Hia moh' is used in Kouega's text to convey the notion of 'having a good feeling'. Hence, 'moh' is synonymous with the Standard English word 'satisfaction' or 'enjoyment'. Another synonym for 'tchouker' used in Kouega's text is 'comb' as in: *"Toi aussi. How tu comb une ngo trois time en un seul day.Tu es became un coq?* (Kouega, 166) [You too. How come you screw a girl three times in a single day? Have you become a cock?] By resorting to different domesticating strategies— codeswitching, semantic shift, compounding, truncation, clipping and reduplication among others Kouega creates a hybrid text that demands of readers to be not just bilingual but also bicultural. A problematizing of translation theory and practice is central to our reading of works by Fouda, Fonkou, and Nganang.

In his text titled *Temps de chien: chronique animale (2001),* translated into English as *Dog Days* (2006) Nganang resorts to the device of language mixing for a myriad of reasons but the rationale he, himself, provides reads as follows:

La rue a une avance singulière tant sur les journalistes que sur les écrivains. Ce roman essaie de se mettre à l'école de la rue.... L'imagination et l'oralité des rues a fabriqué ces personnages qui existent et que j'ai mis dans mon roman (105) [The street exerts a unique pull both on journalists and writers. This novel attempts to depict the street school....The imagination and orality of the street have produced the characters that exist and I have inserted them into my novel.]

In his attempt to transcribe the speech patterns of indigenous Cameroonian populations in French, Nganang switches codes constantly in a bid to make this ex-colonial language bear the weight of the thought patterns of his characters. Code-switching enables him to transpose the imagination, worldview and mannerisms of Cameroonians into standard French as seen in the following excerpt: "Ma woman no fit chasser me for ma long dis-donc! Après tout, ma long na ma long!"(80)[My woman no fit chasser me for ma long, dis donc! Après tout, ma long na ma long!](*Dog Days*, 54) The translator resorted to a *calque* as a translation canon in the passage above. Jones (1997) defines the term 'calque' as "a copy of an original. It is the borrowing of a foreign word or group of words by the literal translation of its components" (53). The translator of Nganang's excerpt did a laudable job of providing an explicatory note in the glossary to shed light on the signification of the statement as follows: "My woman can't throw me out of my house, I tell you! After all, my house is my house!"(208) It is unclear why the translator resorted to a paratext as a translation device instead of inserting the foregoing sentence into the translation itself. Nonetheless, there is no question that the reader of the target text would be deprived of the communicative intent of the novelist had there been no glossary at all. Notice that the word "long" changes grammatical category from adjective to noun in Camfranglais discourse. This style of writing is labeled 'transposition,' a term that Jones (2014) defines as "a translation device which involves a change between grammatical categories, notably nouns, verbs, adjectives, adverbs and prepositions, from the S.L. to the T.L" (77). In Nganang's text, the word '*long*' functions as a noun that refers to the speaker's 'home' or 'residence'. The word 'ma' is a possessive pronoun that the translator has rendered as 'my'.

The foregoing examples lead to the conclusion according to which Nganang's style of writing does not conform with the norms of standard French; this nonconformity could be particularly challenging for translators not familiar with Africanized French. More often than not, the translator had to resort to the technique of exegesis in a bid to surmount seemingly insuperable semantic obstacles as seen in the following excerpt: "*La voix d'un lycéen lui disait: comme d'habitude, Mama Mado. Et ma maîtresse connaissait son goût. La voix d'un autre exigeait, put oya soté, for jazz must do sous-marin.*" (84)[A student's voice would say: the usual, Mama Mado, and my mistress knew just what he wanted. Another's voice would order, put oya soté, for jazz must do sous-marin.](*Dog Days,* 57) Clearly, this passage would constitute a stumbling-block for many a translator. The term "oya" is a Pidgin English word for "oil," in this case oil used in cooking. "Jazz" is a slang word for 'beans.' Kouega (2013) defines *jazz* as "cooked beans usually eaten with 'beignets' at the 'beigetariat'" (210). Cameroonians use the term 'jazz' to describe the trumpet-like sound that one's stomach would make if one ate a lot of beans, or beans that have been poorly prepared. The expression "jazz sous-marin" could be translated as "beans submerged in oil." The sentence above could better be translated into English as: "A student's voice would say: as usual, Mama Mado, and my mistress knew

14

what he wanted. Another's voice would order: put oil so that the jazz look like submarines."[5] The lexeme 'submarines' refers to beans floating on oil. It is noteworthy that in my re-translation of the sentence above I have dropped two words used by the translator that amount to over-translation. The words are "just" and "enough". The reason for eliminating these words is that they have no equivalents in the source text. Wang (2012) defines 'over-translation' as "the information that the target language contains that is more than that of the source language."(131)

As if to make the job of the translator even harder, *Nganang'sTemps de chien* is replete with expressions culled from pidgin English as the following example illustrates: "*Et mon maître lui, se retranchant dans son pidgin de crise, tout en déchirant sur son visage un bleu: Dan sapak i day kan-kan-o.*" (52)[As for my master, he'd fall back into pidgin, his dialect of disaster, cursing the whores as he tore his face into a sick smile: 'Dan sapak i day for kan-kan-o.](*Dog Days*, 35) The code-mixing evident in this excerpt is an indication of Nganang's acknowledgement of the fact that as a writer nurtured in a multilingual context, he is straddling multiple linguistic spheres. Consequently, he spices his text with expressions culled from all the communicative crucibles that constitute his creative font in a bid to make his diction respond realistically to the plurality of codes in which he writes. It should be noted that the word 'sapak' is a term of abuse, generally used in reference to a 'whore'. The expression 'kan-kan', culled from Pidgin English could be translated as 'a variety of'. The word 'day' also derived from Pidgin English translates the Standard English adverb of location, 'there.' The word 'dan' is the pidginized form of the demonstrative adjective 'that'. In *Temps de chien*, recourse to

---

[5] My translation

15

Pidgin English is not to be perceived as an indication of the character's illiteracy or inability to communicate effectively in standard French. Oftentimes, Nganang's characters choose to communicate in pidgin French also called Camfranglais simply as a sign of group solidarity or phatic communion. Echu (2006) observes that the "pidginization processes operational in the two varieties clearly illustrate the relationship between language contact and cultural dynamism, the two speech forms being an expression of the culture of the highly multicultural Cameroonian setting" (1).Given that Nganang's text is deeply embedded in the cultural matrices in which it was conceived the mono-cultural translator would struggle with semantic decipherment.

Code-switching is an effective cross-cultural communication tool in *Temps de chien*. It enables the novelist to express the cultural experiences of Cameroonians in French as seen in the following passage: "Une fois mon maître demanda à Soumi de me donner une part du délicieux koki rouge et huileux qui gonflait son plat." (26) [Once my master asked Soumi to give me some of his delicious red and greasy koki that was piled up in his plate.](*Dog Days*, 17) The rendition of "koki rouge et huileux" as "red and greasy koki" is a barbarism. Koki is not cooked in grease! Koki is the name of a local dish indigenous to some ethnic groups in Cameroon. It is made of ground beans mixed with numerous ingredients steeped in red palm-oil. Nganang's text contains several extra-linguistic elements the meaning of which must be properly deciphered by the translator in order to produce an accurate translation as this excerpt indicates:

> Recroquevillé dorénavant dans son trou obscure de sa crise, mortifié par le souvenir de l'aisance dont il avait été abrupment sevré, émasculé par le bobolo sec aux arachides grillées qu'il

16

devait maintenant manger le matin, à midi et le soir, mon maître ne tendait plus sa main vers moi pour me caresser le crâne.(15) [Hunkered down from then on in the dark hole of his crisis, mortified by memories of the comfortable life from which he has been so abruptly weaned, emasculated by having to eat dry bobolo with grilled peanuts morning, noon and night, my master no longer reached out to caress my head.](*Dog Days*, 10)

'Bobolo' is a dish made of ground cassava wrapped in banana or plantain leaves. A cultural referent such as 'bobolo' may pose translation problems; that is why it is incumbent on the translator to do some research into the genesis of the text s/he is translating in order to unravel the hidden significations of the cultural referents such as the ones discussed above.

Interestingly, several indigenous terms transposed into *Temps de chien* have no French language equivalents. Examples include: "koki" (26), "bobolo" (15), "maguida" (16), "siscia" (112), "ndoutou" and so forth. The term "ndoutou" poses a thorny translation problem as seen in the following passage: "Il frappa ses mains et dit: C'est du ndoutou, dis donc. Elle veut me gâter la journée."(205)[He clapped his hands and said, "It's just ndoutou, I tell you, bad luck. She wants to ruin my day"] (*Dog Days*, 142). It should be noted that 'ndoutou', also spelled 'ndutu', is a camfranglais word that is deemed to be worse than back luck. Fonkoua (2015) notes that "ndutu is misfortune or curse."(190)In Camfranglais discourse it is carries a deeper signification than ill-luck. 'Ndoutou' is a mishap that is likely to ruin one's entire day. This is because there is a myth among Cameroonians according to which a misfortune begets another. For instance, a bayam-sellam (market woman) would tell her first customer to not bring her 'ndoutou' if the customer drove too hard a bargain. The reason is that these women have the conviction that the first customer sets the pace for the day.

Indigenous language words expressions have specific connotations as this excerpt shows: "Des rumta, elles étaient, oui et lui Massa Yo saurait bien les tordre. Il saurait leur montrer qu'il les dépasse. Elles avaient beau être hautains, ces tchotchoro du quartier...." (54)[They are just rumta—and Massa Yo was sure he'd bend them to his will! He'd teach them who was in charge! They could be as haughty as they liked, those local kids—the tchotchoro—he knew how to handle them.] (*Dog Days*, 36) 'Rumta' and 'tchotchoro' are synonymous words that could be translated as "girls in their teens". The words convey the extra-linguistic signification of "green horn" or "inexperienced". The use of these two synonymous words within the same utterance could create hurdles for the translator. Nganang's "Cameroonization" of the French language provides a cultural backdrop against which his creative writing occurs. The onus rests with the translator to transpose this backdrop into the target text. Some code switches in *Temps de chien* introduce elements of vulgarity into the narrative for the purpose of humor. A good example would be the following passage: "Il se leva sur la pointe des pieds et maudit par-dessus la tête de tout le monde la femme qui avait osé le découvrir en public: Youa mami pima!"(222)[He got up on his tiptoes and, shouting over every one's head, cursed the woman who'd dared to expose him in public: "Youa mami pima!"](*Dog Days*, 154) 'Youa mami pima!' is a swear expression. Literally, it means "your mother's vagina!" The translator's task is to look for an equivalent expression in the target language that conveys the same degree of vulgarity. However, this search may prove abortive if the intended readership of the translator is not receptive to this level of linguistic debasement.

Another expression that translates sexuality and bears lascivious overtones in the novel is "ma din wa" as seen in the following passage: "Je t'ai déjà dit: ma din wa. Je sais que tu n'aimes que l'argent, mais moi je t'aime."(231)[I've already told you, ma din wa, I love you. I know you love money, but I still love you.] (*Dog Days*, 161) 'Ma din wa' is an expression culled from the Beti language. It could be translated as 'I love you'as the translator indicated in the glossary (208). Uttered by a whore, the expression would carry ironic undertones because it is devoid of affection given the pecuniary motive behind the love affair. As a matter of fact, Cameroonian prostitutes employ this expression as a euphemism for 'I love your money'. Nganang artfully weaves vernacular turns of phrase into his narrative as these examples illustrate.

Temps de chien is a "Cameroonized" French language text that becomes less and less standardized and quite often draws from several registers. To translate Mboudjak's actions and interactions with other characters in the novel, his thoughts, in short, the totality of his experience and existence into the written word, Nganang deems it necessary to alternate codes. He effectively uses the interplay of several codes—standard French, English and Pidgin, and indigenous languages—as a trope for not only foregrounding the idiosyncrasies of characters but also for evaluating their relationships to one another. Sadly enough, this discursive adaptation carries the germ of communication breakdown when translation into another language is undertaken by a translator who fails to carry out the research necessary to produce a faithful translation. This succinct analysis leads to the conclusion that *Temps de chien* is an hybridized text that requires the translator to be both bilingual and cultural.

In *Temps de chien*, linguistic and extralinguistic constituents merge to produce the totality of the message intended by the writer. Situational and role-shifts demand corresponding code-shifts requiring the reader to interpret the text in order to fully

19

comprehend its import. It is evident from the examples discussed above that this writer uses code-switching to represent particular human dimensions within the socio-cultural setting in which he writes. His recourse to code-switching is determined by the roles the characters play in given speech contexts.

Some pidginized expressions in *Temps de chien* harbor sexual innuendos as the following excerpt suggests: *"Quand elle avait disparu au loin, mon maître disait rêveur: Dan tendaison for dan woman na big big hein?"*(69)[When she has disappeared in the distance, my master would say, still dreaming of her ample behind: Dan tendaison for dan woman na big big huh?](*Dog Days*, 47). Notice that once again the translator has opted for a calque as a translation strategy for the second sentence in this excerpt. That is probably because there are several codes enmeshed in this single utterance: standard French, standard English, and Pidgin English. The reduplication of the word 'big' translates the notion of 'extremity' in the discourse of Camanglophones. Echu (2006) posits that "Camfranglais utterances are strongly marked by reduplication, which is the repetition of morphological and lexical elements within an utterance"(8).He further notes that such repetitions emphasize the intensity or duration of an action; express augmentative and diminutive values, or simply constitute an inherent feature of one of the indigenous contact languages. To drive the point home, Echu provides the following examples: *doucement doucement* (very slowly or very gently), *nayor nayor* (very slowly or very gently), *penya penya* (brand new or in very good state), *beaucoup beaucoup* (in great quantity), *un peu un peu* (very little or in very small quantities), *depuis depuis* (a very long time ago)*, nyama nyama* (very small; of little significance or value).

The word "tendaison" used in the excerpt above is the Camfranglais word for "buttocks." In this passage, Mini

20

Minor's buttocks are depicted as extremely big. The sentence could be translated as: "When she had disappeared in the distance, my master would say, still dreaming of her ample behind: That woman has extremely big buttocks, huh?" It should be noted that the translator drew a blank when it came to translating the last segment of this utterance: "Dan tendaison for dan woman na big big huh?" With the exception of the word 'hein' which she rendered as 'huh', the utterance was simply transposed into the target text, thus leaving the target language reader in a quandary. A similar translation anomaly is noticeable in the translator's abortive attempt to render the following excerpt:

> *Femme, avait-il dit, tu n'as pas entendu ce qu'on raconte? Les voleurs*
> *ont déjà la potion pour se rendre invisibles ici dehors. N'est-ce pas hier ils*
> *sont entrés dans le salon de Massa Kokari et ont emporté sa télévision sous*
> *son nez? A di tell you!* (50)
> [Woman, he said, haven't you heard what people are saying? Thieves already have a potion that makes them invisible out there. Don't you know that yesterday they went into Massa Kokari's living room and took his television right from under his nose? A di tell you!] (*Dog Days*, 34).

The emphatic Pidgin English expression, "A di tell you!" could be translated as: "Take it from me!" Instead, the translator opted for a calque. Generally speaking, Cameroonians employ an expression like this in a bid to dispel doubt, especially when they sense disbelief on the part of the interlocutor. The word "massa" is the pidginized equivalent of the Standard English word "Mr."or "Master". These expressions are germane in Nganang's text given they speak to the polyglossia that characterizes fictional writing in the Camfranglais context. Each linguistic variety invokes a specific type of discourse that is in synchrony with the social stratus of the speaker(s). The style in which *Temps de chien* is written amounts to a wedding of a European language—in our case French, with indigenous languages. This mode of writing is not the preserve of Nganang.

In her novel titled *Je parle camerounais: pour un revouveau francofaune* (2001), Mercédès Fouda follows in the footsteps of her compatriot by jettisoning the yoke of linguistic imperialism through the process of indigenization of language as seen in the following excerpt:

> Le gombo, c'est ce petit job périodique et sporadique dont les revenus disparaissent aussi rapidement que son homonyme, plante mucilagineuse dont on fait les sauces, et qui, surtout cuisinée avec du couscous, descend à toute vitesse dans la gorge (36) [Gombo is this menial job that one gets occasionally whose revenue disappears as rapidly as its floral homonym, plant used in making soup which descends with ease down the gullet, especially when eaten with fufu.]

It should be noted that the term 'gombo' refers to 'okra'. However, in this context it is used as an equivalent of the English language word 'windfall'. The task of the translator in instances like these resides in distinguishing the literal from the figurative usage of terms and expressions used by the creative writer to communicate specific semantic shifts.Fouda constantly shifts meaning for the purpose of transcribing the speech patterns of Cameroonians into French as this example illustrates: *"Ces temps derniers les jeunes talents se sont vus affubler des substantives "yo" et "yoyettes," surtout s'ils se sont branchés comme des fils électriques, avec pantalons en tire-bouchon…"* (62) [Lately, these youngsters have gotten into the habit of referring to each other as "yo"and "yoyettes", especially when they are dressed to the nines and look like electric poles.] The standard French words 'jeune' and 'talent' have been endowed with entirely new significations, especially when collocated as is the case in this context. It is worth mentioning that words such as "yo" and "yoyettes" are culled from Cameroonian indigenous languages. Both words describe young boys and girls that are smartly dressed. Kouega (2013) provides the following definition for the term 'yo': "a lad; a young boy that dresses well" (319). As far as the term 'yoyette' is concerned, he provides the following definition: "a young lady, a young girl that dresses well" (319). Kouega provides the following example to shed more light: "La yoyette-là a put une belle dress au day" [That young lady is wearing a very beautiful dress today] (319). Unfamiliarity with the etymology and contextual usage of these words may render the task of the translator painstaking. The linguistic appropriation process that transpires in *Je parle camerounais* has the potential of making the text hard to translate by a non-Cameroonian translator on account of the cultural specificity of the lexical items chosen by the writer.

The language manipulation that occurs in Fouda's narrative speaks volumes about the author's conscious attempt to translate orality into the written word; to domesticate the French language for the purpose of expressing an indigenous worldview and self-identity. In this vein, literary scholar, Ojo-Ade (1986), makes the following pertinent remarks:

On the whole, one may safely say that the dual culture of the African writer (the native culture he is writing about and the European culture he has imbibed) makes him first and foremost a translator before being a creative artist. ("The Role of the Translator,"295)

One may deduce from Ojo-Ade's remarks that the translation of indigenous imagination and cultural relativity into European languages remains a salient feature of

Camfranglais literature. Thinking along similar lines, Gyasi (1999) posits that contemporary fictional writing in Francophone Africa is "a creative translation process that leads to the production of a …text in French and the development of an authentic African discourse."(151) All too often, Fouda spices her text with expressions that reflect the Cameroonian discourse, a trope that defy comprehensibility by translators who do not belong in the closed circle of Camfranglais speakers as seen in the following passage: *"Si depuis belle lurette vous vous démenez de-ci de-là sans trouver aucune occasion à saisir sur le plan matériel, vous pourrez toujours vous plaindre que le dehors est dur…"* (5). [If you have been searching here and there in vain for a job to make ends meet, you could always complain that times are hard.] "Le dehors est dur" is a Cameroonianism[6] that translates the idea that times are hard. There is no denying the fact that an understanding of the contextual usage of Cameroonianisms employed in Fouda's *Je parle camerounais* would serve to enlarge the translators' comprehension of the text and make it more accessible than it would be if they were to know nothing of the circumstances surrounding the creation of the text. Fonkou's *Moi taximan* (2001) harbors similar hurdles. *Moi taximan* seems to defy translation on account of code-mixing and the Africanization of French language as the following sentence shows:

J'avais remarqué dès les premiers jours que certains collègues clandos ne s'arrêtaient pas aux barrières de contrôle, ou que quand ils s'y arrêtaient, c'était pour échanger avec les contrôleurs des plaisanteries puis repartir sans avoir servi ni le café ni la bière. (12)

[I had noticed from the onset that some clando colleagues never stopped at the police checkpoint, or only stopped there to

---

[6] Speech patterns and discursive mannerism typical of Cameroonians

crack jokes with the officials and leave without serving coffee or beer].

Fonkou's recourse to the word 'clando' is likely to pose comprehension problems for the literary translator because it is a Camfranglais neologism derived from the word 'clandestine'. The thing that makes the task of the translator even more daunting is the fact that 'clando' has been assigned a new signification through the process of semantic shift. Kouega (2013) defines 'clando' as "a private car illegally used as a taxi."(164) 'Clando' also refers to a taxi driven by a driver who does not possess the legal documentation that grants him or her the right to drive a taxi. Sometimes, Cameroonians use the word 'clando' to describe a private car used to transport passengers illegally. This elucidation lends credibility to the fact that the task of translating literature written in Camfranglais calls for an interpretative approach. Without some background knowledge of the word formative processes that transpire in Camfranglophone discourses, it would be difficult, if not impossible, for the translator to unravel the hidden significations of the literature he or she is attempting to translate.

Fonkou resorts to the technique of compounding in an attempt to acquaint his readers with the thought patterns of Camfranglais speakers: "*Les premiers contacts avec les mange-mille et les gendarmes coûtent cher, mais par la suite, tout le monde se connaît et il s'établit comme un contrat tacite*"(12). [The first encounters with the mange-mille and gendarmes often cost much, but with time, people get to know one another and a sort of tacit contract is established.] It noteworthy that 'mange-mille' is a Camfranglais derogatory term used in Cameroon to describe corrupt police officers who are prone to taking bribes from commuters. The linguistic tinkering that is noticeable in Fonkou's style of

25

creative writing gives his literature local color which could be the translator's nightmare at the same time. The French used by Fonkou in this novel has been described as "le français langue africaine" [African French] by Cameroonian socio-linguist, Mendzo Zé (1999). Some Camfranglais lexical items are hard to decipher by a translator who is unaccustomed to the lexicon of this new urban slang. As Nstobé et al. (2008) would have it, *'Il faut absolument connaître la signification de ces mots dans leurs contextes spécifiques*" (90) [You really have to know the meanings and contextual usage of these words.] The difficulty of mastering the contextual usage of these newly created words stems from the fact that camfranglophones frequently borrow words and expressions from indigenous languages to embellish their parlance as this proverbial expression shows: "L'Enfant qui vit près de la chefferie ne craint pas le 'mekwum'" (14). [The child who lives near the palace does not fear the 'mekwum'] The word 'mekwum' is an indigenous language word that refers to a masked dancer belonging in a village secret society.[7] The following excerpt is rich in borrowings from vernacular languages spoken in Cameroon:

Dès que je me trouvais au milieu de cette foule ce furent d'interminables poignées de mains d'une vigueur à vous déséquilibrer, d'interminable 'nge pin', 'a pon', 'a bha'a, toutes les expressions de l'approbation et de la satisfaction.(93) [As soon as I found myself in this crowd, we shook hands incessantly and so vigorously that one could lose one's equilibrium, endless 'nge pin', 'a pon', 'a bha'a, expressions of approbation and satisfaction.]

---

[7] occultist group

The foregoing discourse analysis lends itself to two seminal conclusions. First, Camfranglais fictional works are not canonical texts; rather they belong in the category of peripheral ethnographic texts that require an interpretive approach to literary criticism. Camfranglais fiction exists at an intersection of French as an imperial language and its regional variant on account of linguistic appropriation that often engenders a third code— Camfranglais.

In an attempt to convey Cameroonian socio-cultural specificities, worldviews, imagination and sensibilities in a European language, in our case French, Camfranglais fiction writers consciously deconstruct French in a bid to fabricate a new language. Second, taking into cognizance the multilayered substratum from which Camfranglais literature derives its special qualities, translators would fare better if they had recourse to multidimensional frameworks in a bid to accomplish faithful translation—one such model, namely the *Hermeneutic-Exegetic model* is discussed in the following chapter.

Chapter Three

Toward a Hermeneutic-Exegetic Model of Translation

According to Anthony Pym (1995), *Hermeneutics* or the theory of interpretation was propounded by Friedrich Schleiermacher in his lecture titled "On the Different Methods of Translation"[8] delivered to the Royal Academy of Science on June 24, 1813. To paraphrase Pym, energetic, systematic, and fecund, Schleiermacher' theory underscores the importance of interpreting, not just the latent (hidden) significations embedded in a literary text but also the situational dimensions that constitute the matrix in which the text was conceived. Schleiermacher puts emphasis on the importance of the hermeneutic circle as an indispensable foothold in the exegetic interpretation of meanings embedded in the deep structure of the literary text. The hermeneutic circle supports and facilitates the critical analysis of the literary text by enabling the translator to come to terms with the fact that one's understanding of a text is conditioned by a conscientious engagement with both the linguistic and extralinguistic elements that account for textual holism. Schleiermacher further observes that neither the whole text nor any individual components can be understood without reference to one another, and hence, the notion of a circle. The circularity inherent in hermeneutics lends itself readily to usage in the translation of literature written in Camfranglais because these texts are sociological novels the complete meaning of which can only be unraveled

---

[8] Das Problem des Übersetzens, edited by Hans Joachim Störig (Darmstadt, 1963), pp. 38-70. 2.

by taking cognizance of their cultural, historical, temporal and spatial constituents.

The *hermeneutic* theory goes hand in hand with the theory of *exegesis* in translation studies because the science of interpretation is integral to the theory and practice of translation. According to Margot (1975) serious exegetical study of the source text is a prerequisite for producing a translation of high quality..." (156). He further points out that translations are like women: if they are beautiful they are not faithful, if they are faithful they are not beautiful. *Exegesis* is understood to mean a thorough analysis of the content of a text for translation purposes. Textual analysis is not limited to the unraveling of meaning encapsulated by linguistic components; rather it englobes both verbal and non-verbal constituents of the source text. An exegetic approach to translation entails the translator's conscious effort to unearth the significations embedded in the source text in its wider literary, historical, geographical and cultural contexts. In other words, the translator must constantly ask questions such as: What am I translating? For whom am I translating? Where and when am I translating? Why am I translating what I am translating? In doing so, translators must endeavor to rid themselves of shackles imposed by the quest for formal correspondence. The *Hermeneutic- Exegetic* translation model that we propose in this book is a sine qua non for success in translating literature written in less commonly taught languages such as Camfranglais because this sort of literature is not just pluri-linguistic; it is multicultural as well. The *Hermeneutic-Exegetic* paradigm is analogous to cultural adaptation, a translation mode that enables the translator to comprehend the nuanced cultural significations of the source text. Steiner (1975) observes that the hermeneutic-exegetic approach to translation sees the relationship between translation and translator as an act of interpretation. As he puts it, "the translator-interpreter creates a condition of significant exchange" (318). *Hermeneutics* deals with the ways in which the translator discovers meaning embedded in the situational dimensions of the source text. Viewed from this perspective, *Hermeneutics* is a kind of semantic discernment process; ways of mining the holistic meaning of the original text, as it were. On the other hand, *exegesis* is a method of attempting to understand a text. The exegete studies the lexical meanings and grammar of the source text in order to discern that which the author intended to convey. *Exegesis* entails applying various rules of interpretation to a given text in a bid to expound and reveal the essence of its message(s). In the two-pronged Hermeneutic-Exegetic translation process, the translator strives to understand what led to the writing of the text, and what circumstances prevailed during the author's time of writing. In sum, the Hermeneutic-Exegetic process is both deductive and inductive. Induction involves three processes, namely observation, interpretation and application.

In Chapter Four, we intend to put the validity and practicability of the aforementioned model to the test by translating an excerpt from Fouda's *Je parle camerounais: pour un renouveau francofaune* (2001) as well as excerpts from two of Vakunta's books of poems written in Camfranglais, namely *Speak Camfranglais pour un renouveau ongolais* (2014) and *Requiem pour Ongola en camfranglais: une poétique camerounaise* (2015). In our translation of the aforementioned corpus, we intend to remain as faithful as possible to the holistic meaning of the source texts. Structural adjustments will be made in the target texts when deemed necessary. In each case, explanations will be provided to shed ample light on the rationale behind deviance from the formal configuration of the source texts. Most importantly, problems encountered during the translation process will be explicated. Emphasis will be placed on

31

translation approaches that were employed by the translator in
a bid to surmount communicative bottle-necks.

Chapter Four

Validation of the Model (Translation Excerpts)

Excerpt from Mercédès Fouda's *Je parle camerounais: pour un renouveau francofaune* (2001)

"Manger en Ville" (pp. 9-14)

Depuis le temps que vous discouriez, la petite aiguille et la trotteuse de votre montre ont eu l'occasion de se positionner sur le chiffre de 12. Midi, l'heure d'aller manger un peu, car "votre estomac vous lance des insultes", autrement dit vous mourez de faim; ici l'homme de la rue dira qu'il va "manger midi", le "midi" étant le nom donné à tout repas pris dans l'intervalle de 12 à 14 heures.

Pour vous restaurer, vous avez le choix : il y a tout d'abord les "cafétariats"; peu de citoyens savent qu'il s'agit d'une cafétéria, à l'origine italienne, mais à quoi bon s'évertuer à corriger? Et puis, si le prolétariat est le statut du prolétaire, et le notariat celui du notaire, pourquoi le "cafétariat" ne serait-il pas celui du cafétier?

Vous débarquezdonc dans ce petit local en planches et vous vous enquérez du menu: il ne dispose que d'"oeufs frits", conventionnellement appelés "omelette", et d'un fond de "jazz". Le jazz est cette légumineuse de nom commun "haricot", musicalement appellée ainsi parce l'ingestion de ce protoide azoté provoque chez le consommateur des fuites sonores ressemblant a s'y méprendre au son d'une trompette. Lorsque les haricots sont recouverts d'huile, on les qualifie de " jazz sous-marin". Ce qui vous dégoûte, car si vous aimez que "tout baigne", cela ne s'applique pas aux haricots.

33

Vous avez alors la possibilité d'aller manger au "tournedos".
Ne vous réjouissez pas trop vite! Vous n'irez que dans l'un de
ces restaurants de plein air, faits de bancs et de tables assemblés,
et où tout bêtement, le client tourne le dos à la route!
Au tournedos, officie l'"asso". L'"asso", diminutif flatteur
de "associé(e), est cette personne chez qui vous faites
régulièrement des achats et qui, lorsque c'est "fort sur vous",
vous fait "manger un crédit", un repas que vous paeirez plus tard;
c'est d'ailleurs ce que vous escomptez aujourd'hui, puisque,
comme l'on a dit, vous ne "voyez pas du bien".

Il faut préciser que quand l' "asso" est une femme, on lui
confère le doux nom de "mamie", immédiatement suivi du nom
de la recette qu'elle réussit le mieux.on retrouve ainsi des
"mamies koki", le "koki" étant ce mets de haricots blancs
écrasés, mélangés avec de l'huile de palme et cuits à l'étouffe; on
entendra aussi des "mami ndolè" ou des "mami atchomo"…

Vous arrivez donc au tournedos, vous prenez place à côté
des consommateurs déjà installés et vous souhaitez poliment
"appétit!". Certains vous jetteront des regards peu amènes,
comme si vous aviez tué leur père, et les plus aimables vous
répondront "à grand!", l'histoire de faire comprendre que devant
votre "appétit", il manque un "bon", surtout qu'il y a une nette
propension à l'ellipse de l'accent aigu de "appétit". Vous devrez
rectifier immédiatement.

Donc , après vous être installé sur une minuscule portion de
banc bringuebalant, vous lancez négligemment;
_ Mamie, fais-moi le "beau-regard" ou l'"oiseau".
_ Le "beau-regard" et l' "oiseau"sont finis, il ne reste que la
"viande", rétorque mamie "folong".
Que signifient donc si sibyllines syllabes?
Tout simplement que vous avez demandé qu'on vous serve
de la viande de porc ou du poulet.

L'expression "faire" est utilisée dans le contexte commercial pour "vendre" ou "servir"; si donc le vendeur, dans un magasin, s'enquiert:

"Je vous fais un dentrifice?, ne pensez pas qu'il ira d'abord fabriquer la pâte au fluor et le tube.

Le porc est qualifié de "beau-regard" parce que les autochtones lui trouvent le regard doux et séduisant des myopes.

Le terme de "viande" désigne celle de boeuf: si vous arrivez dans quelque tournedos, et qu'après avoir "gourmandement" ouvert les marmites—boeuf, porc, singe, sanglier, porc-épic, crocodile, défieront alors vos facultés olfactives—vous choisissez, en pointant du doigt, le crocodile, ne commettez point l'erreur de dire:

"Asso, fais-moi du riz avec cette viande!" car, même si vous avez clairement désigné la chair de votre goût, asso vous servira du boeuf; aussi devrez-vous toujours indiquer votre choix par le nom de l'animal ex-clu-si-ve-ment. Vous direz:

_Mamie, je voudrais du porc-épic!, point final, parce que, en réclamant "de la viande de porc-épic", vous risquez de vous retrouver avec deux morceaux , l'un de boeuf et l'autre de porc-épic.

Or, le temps passe, le temps passe, les plats survolent votre tête, atterrissant devant les autres clients, même les nouveaux venus, et vous êtes là avec "zéro assiette". "Zéro" est mis devant un substantif pour en siginifier l'absence: une femme stérile, c'est pénible mais c'est ainsi, a donc "zéro enfant", mais elle vous intéresse pour l'instant moins que votre propre malheur de ne pas encore être servi.

_Mais asso, tu m'oublies?protesterez-vous rapidement, inquiet du niveau d'étiage dans les marmites de sauce.

_ Comment tu me fais comme ça? répondra la grosse femme en fuyant votre regard.

Traduction déplaisante de cette phrase ambiguë: "ô! Mon ami (je n'ai pas d'envie de t'accorder un crédit aujourd'hui) pourquoi me places-tu devant ce cas de conscience? Va t'en, je serai beaucoup plus tranquille!..."

C'est donc en ces termes que l'on vous refusera quelque chose, car, paradoxalement, ils sont utilisés par la personne qui ne consent pas au service. Par exemple, vous avez besoin d'argent et vous vous dirigez tout naturellement droit au bureau d'un ami pour lui exposer votre "pro", problème, pendant trois quarts d'heure. Cet ami subitement très affairé, s'occupe avec une ferveur inhabituelle d'un dossier étique. Si vous prenez l'initiative d'insister, et que cet ami vous rétorque "comment tu me fais comme ça?" considérez que c'est un refus et débarrassez le plancher.

Seulement, aujourd'hui, chez "mamie ntouba", vous avez une faim de loup et nullement l'intention de partir sans avoir mangé. Vous redemandez avec indécence:

_Dis donc mamie, c'est comment?

Comme elle n'est nullement de bonne humeur aujourd'hui, elle vous jettera sans douceur:

_Ha! Ne me " tensionne " pas hein? Exigeant de la sorte que vous ne l'énerviez point, ou plus exactement, que vous n'augmentiez pas l'état de tension dans lequel elle se trouve déjà. Indigné, vous dites alors:

_Comme ça? question signifiant toujours dans le contexte d'une dispute: "C'est à moi que tu fais une chose pareille?"

Et dans la foulée, vous vous levez brusquement en annonçant votre futur boycott.

_ Tu vas encore me voir ici!

On comprend donc que vous ne reviendrez plus jamais, car les termes sous-entendent exactement le contraire de ce qu'ils affirment. La preuve, si une fille se fait courtiser par un quidam qui ne lui plaît pas, et qu'elle lui accorde un rendez-vous vite fait pour s'en débarrasser, elle ira plus tard confier à sa copine:

_ Il va me voir à son rendez-vous, manifestant ainsi la ferme intention de ne pas s'y rendre.

Au tournedos,de deux choses l'une:

1. Soit vous quittez immédiatement la scène, furieux, honteux et affamé, poursuivi par un "va même avec ta malchance", en guise de bon débarras, qui est jeté aux personnes de mauvais caractère, risquant de créer du grabuge. Un supporter ennemi appréciera certainement auprès de "mamie vipère":

_ Ma soeur, tu lui as fait "Annaba".

Le bougre a bien raison , puisque "faire Annaba" à quelqu'un, c'est lui infliger la grande honte de sa vie. Ceci provenant de ce que les "Lions Indomptables", équipe nationale de football du Cameroun, s'étaient fait rosser de façon peu honorable lors d'une competition internationale à Annaba en Algérie. Quand "on fait Annaba" à quelqu'un, il peut "rentrer dans sa poche" parce qu'il est mort de honte.

2.Soit "Asso", decidement de mauvaise humeur, n'en a cure et répond ainsi à votre menace de secession:

_Et puis? Tu craches je mange?

"Tu craches, je mange?" est approprié pour faire savoir qu'on se fiche pas mal de son interlocuteur, parce qu'on ne vit pas à ses crochets, de même qu'on peut reprocher ainsi à un fanfaron de vouloir jouer les personnages trop importants.

Pareille imprudence de la part de Mamie vous met hors de vous; vous hurlez d'autant plus rageusement que votre estomac se fait de en plus menaçant:

_ Tu crois même que tu es quoi?

Non mais pour qui se prend-elle?

_Fiche! Fait-elle avec un geste méprisant de la main, comme si elle chassait une mouche, pour que vous la laissiez en paix, et si elle est inspirée, elle pourra ajouter:

_ Sors de mes yeux! que vous traduisez sans peine par "hors de ma vue!", comprenant que "mamie sanga", votre associée de tous les jours , vous enjoint brutalement de partir.

English Translation

"Eating in Town"

You've been talking for a while now and the minute and hour hands of your wrist-watch have had the chance to position themselves on the number 12. It is midday; time to go find a little something to eat because "your stomach is hauling insults at you." In other words, you're starving. Any ordinary Joe would say he's going to "eat his midday", midday being the name given to any meal eaten between noon and 2:00p.m. To feed yourself, you've got a number of locations to choose from: first, there are "cafetariats"; very few citizens are aware of the fact that this term refers to cafeteria, a word of Italian origin. But why waste time correcting them? If the proletariat refers to the status of the proletarian, and the notariat that of the notary, why would cafetariat not refer to the status of a café owner?

So, you show up at these small premises made out of planks, and you ask for the menu: they only have "fried eggs", conventionally called "omelette", and a small quantity of "jazz". "Jazz" is this leguminous plant commonly known as "beans", now musically re-baptized because the ingestion of this nitrogenous protein causes consumers to pass air so loudly that one could mistake the noise for the sound of a trumpet. When jazz is submerged in oil, it's called "submarine jazz". This is

38

rather disgusting because if you love "full baths", this does not apply to beans.

So you have the opportunity to go eat at the "tournedos. "Don't get too excited! You will only find yourself at one of these open-air restaurants where benches and tables are assembled for clients to sit and sheepishly turn their backs to the street! At the tournedos, the "asso" is in charge. "Asso" is the flattering abbreviation for "associate"—the person from whom you buy stuff on a regular basis—and who would let you "eat a credit"[9] and pay for your meal later if you had a hard time making ends meet. Indeed, this is what you're banking on today because as already mentioned, you're not "seeing clearly" as they say.

Let's make it clear that when the "asso" is a woman, she's given the endearing epithet "mamie" which is appended to the name of the meal which she is adept at preparing. Thus, there is "mami koki", "koki" being a dish composed of crushed white beans steeped in palm oil and steamed in a tightly shut steamer . You'd also hear appellations such as "mamie ndole" ou "mamie atchomo"…

So you arrive at the tournedos, and take a seat next to other eaters who are already seated. You politely wish them "appetite!" Some of them look at you in a very unpleasant way as if you had murdered their father, and those who are more amiable answer you with "same to grand!" This is their way of letting you know that you omitted the qualifier "good", especially given the strong tendency of folks to elide the acute accent on the word "appetite". You have to correct the error instantly.

So after occupying a tiny portion of the wobbly bench, you nonchalantly place your order:

"Mamie, do me some "good looks" or "bird."

---

[9] Buy on credit

"We're out of "good looks" and bird. Only "meat" is left," says Mamie "folong"

So what do these enigmatic syllables signify? This means that you've requested that they serve you some pork and chicken.

The verb "do" is used in the commercial context to mean "sell" or "serve". So if a salesperson in a shop asks you:

"May I do you some toothpaste? Don't think that he's going to first of all manufacture the fluoridated paste and tube.

Pork is referred to as "good looks" because local folks believe that the gentle and seductive looks of pigs can be likened to the looks of the near-sighted. The term "meat" refers to meat from cows: as such if you got to any tournedos and eagerly opened the pots, your olfactory faculties would be tickled by the aroma emanating from beef, pork, monkey, wild boar, porcupine, crocodile—and you'd make your choice by pointing at the crocodile—do not commit the blooper of saying:

"Asso, do me some rice and this meat!" If you say that, the asso will serve you beef, even if you'd clearly indicated the flesh of your choice. So you've to always indicate your choice by ex-clu-sive-ly specifying the name of the animal. Thus, you'd say:

"Mamie, I would love to have some porcupine, period! If you ask for porcupine meat, you may wind up with two pieces—one beef and the other porcupine.

Anyhow, time passes, time passes, plates are flying over your head and landing in front of other clients, even newcomers and you're sitting there with "zero plate." " Zero" is placed in front of any substantive to indicate absence of: so a sterile woman, it's painful but it is what it is, has "zero child", but at this moment her plight is less important to you than your own mishap of not having been served yet.

"But, have you forgotten about me?" This is your way of protesting, worried as you are about the low level of soup in the pots.

40

"Why are you doing this to me?" That's the manner in which the fat woman would respond to you, trying to avoid eye contact.

This unpleasant statement couched in ambiguity could be translated as follows: "O! My friend (I have no desire at all to let you eat on credit today), why are putting me in this embarrassing situation? Go away; I shall feel a lot more at ease!"

So, these are the words that are used when someone refuses to render you services, because, paradoxically, they are uttered by the person who refuses to grant a request. For instance, you need some money and make your way unaffectedly to a friend's office in order to apprize him of your "pro", problem. For three quarters of an hour, this friend, who suddenly looks terribly busy, is paying unusual attention to a scraggy file. If you take the initiative to insist and this friend of yours replies: "why are you doing this to me?" you must understand that he has refused to help you; and you must decamp.

The trouble is that today, at "Mamie Ntouba's tournedos, you're starving and have no intention at all to leave without eating. So, you reiterate your request indecently:

"Look here Mamie, what's all this?"

Since she is not at all in a good mood today, she'll answer you back harshly:

"Ha! Don't cause me 'tension' hein?" This is her way of telling you not to get on her nerves at all, or to put it more bluntly, you should not dare raise the tension in which she already finds herself. Outraged you'd answer:

"Like that?" In the context of a disagreement, this question would be translated as: "Who would believe you're doing this to me?"

While you're at it, you stand up abruptly and announce your departure as follows:

"You're going to see me here again!"

It is understood that you'll never set foot there again, because your statement implies the exact opposite of what you mean. A case in point: if a girl agrees to honor a date with a man she doesn't like because he has been pestering her, she would go to her friend later and say:

"He's going to see me at that date of his; this translates her firm determination to not honor the date.

At the tournedos, one of two things may happen:

(1) You leave the scene immediately, feeling angry, ashamed and hungry, followed by words such as "spare us your ill-luck", a way of saying good riddance, an expression that is tossed at ill-mannered people who tend to create havoc. An adversary, clearly friendly to "Mamie viper", would say:

"My sister, you've served him 'Annaba.'"

The guy is quite right because to "serve someone Annaba" is to bring on that person the worst humiliation of their life. This saying stems from the terrible experience of the Indomitable Lions, national soccer team of Cameroon, who were humiliated with a defeat during an international competition at Annaba in Algeria. When someone "is given Annaba" they can enter their pocket because they are dying of shame.

(2) Asso, clearly in a bad mood, couldn't care less and reacts to your threat to secede as follows:

"So what? Do I drink your spit?"

"Do I drink your spit?" is an appropriate expression to use when you want to let your interlocutor understand that you couldn't care less because you do not sponge off anyone. This expression also comes in handy when you want to deflate the ego of a braggart who tries to pass off as a big shot.

This sort of effrontery from Mamie really pisses you off and you scream as furiously as your stomach which is threating you more and more:

"Who do you even think you are?"

For heaven's sake, who does she think she is?

"Piss off!" Says Mamie followed by a disdainful hand gesture that gives the impression that she's chasing off a fly. This is her way of asking you to leave her alone. If she's inspired, she may add:

"Get out of my eyes!" And you'd understand that she's asking you to get "out of her sight!" In other words, "Mamie Sanga," your associate forever is telling you rudely to leave.

Excerpt from PeterVakunta's *Speak Camfranglais pour un renouveau ongolais* (2014)

"Hyme camerien" (pp.57-63)

Mes complices de Nkouloulou-o!
Ma complice dem for Nkouloulou-o!
Mes taras de Mokolo-o!
Ma tara dem for Mokolo-o!
Ma mombo dem for Marché central-o!
Mes amis du Marché central-o!
Ma kombi dem for Kumba market-o!
Mes potes au Marché de Kumba-o!
Ma dong pipo dem for Kasala farm-o!
Les sauveteurs du Kasala farm-o!
Da wan dem for Camp Sic de Bassa-o!
Ceux du Camp Sic de Yabassi-o!

Sep da wan dem for ngata for Tchollire-o!
Même ceux qui purgent des peines
Au sein de la prison de Tchollire-o!
De wan dem for Robben Island de Kondengui,
Ceux qui végètent dans la prison

43

Cauchemardesque de Kondengui
Ala wan em for prison de Mantoum-o!
Les autres en prison de Bamenda-o !
Sep da wan dem for Buea!

Laissez-moi vous langua cette nouvelle.
I sei mek I langua wuna dis tori.
Un nouvel hymne national vient de naître à Ongola.
Some national anthem dong commot
Just now for Ongola.
Da mean say some national anthem
Dong show head for we own kontri.
Voici comment se chante notre hymne national:

Le Cameroun c'est le cameroun,
On va faire comment alors?
That is to say,
Cameroon is Cameroon,
What can we do?
In ala word,
Cameroon na Cameroon,
We go do na how-no ?

Grand Katika d'Etoudi,
Kick all ndou for caisses de l'Etat,
On chante toujours :
Le Cameroun c'est le Cameroun,
On va faire comment alors ?
That is to say,
Cameroon is Cameroon,
What can we do?
In ala word,
Cameroon na Cameroon,

44

We go do na how-no ?

Les ministres détournent leurs mbourous de l'Etat,
On chante sans cesse:
Le Cameroun c'est le Cameroun,
On va faire comment alors ?
That is to say,
Cameroon is Cameroon,
What can we do?
In ala word,
Cameroon na Cameroon,
We go do na how-no ?

Les zangalewa matraquent
Les étudiants en grève sur le campus
De l'Université de Buea, jusqu'à les nyoxer,
On chante comme d'hatibude:
Le Cameroun c'est le Cameroun,
On va faire comment alors ?
That is to say,
Cameroon is Cameroon,
What can we do?
In ala word,
Cameroon na Cameroon,
We go do na how-no?

Les mange-mille meng les taximan
Parcequ'ils ont refusé de choko,
On chante seulement:
Le Camer c'est le Camer,
On va faire comment alors ?
That is to say,
Cameroon is Cameroon,

What can we do?
In ala word,
A Cameroonian is a Cameroonian,
We go do na how-no ?

Les gendarmes violent les bayam sellam
Parce qu'elles ne veulent pas donner le café,
On chante sans cesse:
Le Cameroun c'est le cameroun,
On va faire comment alors ?
That is to say,
Cameroon is Cameroon,
What can we do?
In ala word,
Cameroon na Cameroon,
We go do na how-no ?

Les hommes politiques
Truquent les élections à vue d'oeil,
Parce qu'ils sont affligés de la mégalomanie,
On chante:
L'Ongola c'est l'Ongola,
On va faire comment alors ?
That is to say,
Cameroon is Cameroon,
What can we do?
In ala word,
Cameroon na Cameroon,
We go do na how-no ?

Le ngomna refuse de goudronner les routes,
Parce que les ministres ont tout kick,

On chante sans avoir honte:
Le Cameroun c'est le cameroun,
On va faire comment alors ?
That is to say,
Cameroon is Cameroon,
What can we do?
In ala word,
Cameroon na Cameroon,
We go do na how-no ?

Les fonctionnaires sont compressés
A cause de la crise économique
Et la corruption endémique,
Engendrée par le dysfonctionnement étatique,
On chante:
Le Cameroun c'est le cameroun,
On va faire comment alors ?
That is to say,
Cameroon is Cameroon,
Na so da we own
Cameroon National Anthem dei!

What can we do?
In ala word,
Cameroon na Cameroon,
We go do na how-no ?
Na so da we own
Hymne ongolais dei!

Les diplômés d'université
Se retrouvent au Chomencam,
On chante comme des moutons :
Le Cameroun c'est le cameroun,

On va faire comment alors?
That is to say,
Cameroon is Cameroon,
Na so da we own
Cameroon National Anthem dei!

Le Grand Katika nous largue
Une constitution constipée
Bekoz il veut crever au pouvoir,
On chante bêtement,
Pour ne pas dire moutonnement:
Le Cameroun c'est le cameroun,
On va faire comment alors ?
That is to say,
Cameroon is Cameroon,
Na so da we own
Cameroon National Anthem dei!

Les Mbere-Khaki meng
Bendskinneurs foreska affaire nkap,
On chante:
Le Cameroun c'est le cameroun,
On va faire comment alors?
That is to say,
Cameroon is Cameroon,
Na so da we own
Cameroon National Anthem dei!

Le Chop Pipo Dem Moni party(CPDM)
Nous fait voir de toutes les couleurs,
Parce qu'il n'y a pas moyen
Pour les partis d'opposition ongolais d'y faire face,
On chante comme des cinglés:

Le Cameroun c'est le cameroun,
On va faire comment alors?
That is to say,
Cameroon is Cameroon,
Na so da we own
Cameroon National Anthem dei!

Le Grand Katika sort tout l'argent
De la Caisse noire présidentielle
Afin d'aller construire
Son hôpital privé à Baden-Baden
On chante peureusement:
Le Cameroun c'est le cameroun,
On va faire comment alors ?
That is to say,
Cameroon is Cameroon,
Na so da we own
Cameroon National Anthem dei!
Une wolowoss se métamorphose en Première Dame
On chante:
Le Cameroun c'est le cameroun,
On va faire comment alors ?
That is to say,
Cameroon is Cameroon,
Na so da we own
Cameroon National Anthem dei!

Un professeur ongolais dépassé
Par l'état des choses s'écrie :
Vraiment le cameroun est formidable,
Vivons seulement.
Da mean sei:
Cameroon na wandaful

Mek we begin nye daso.
C'est le comble!

English Translation

"Camerian Anthem"

My partners in crime in Nkouloulou-o!
My partners in crime for Nkouloulou-o!
My tara in Mokolo-o!
My tara in Mokolo-o!
My namesakes at the Main Market-o!
My friends at the Main Market-o!
My friends at the Kumba Market-o!
My mates in Kumba Market-o!
My suffering people at the Kasala farm-o!
The sauveteurs in Mbanga-o!
Those at the Camp Sic Bassa-o!
Those at Camp Sic Yabassi-o!

Even those who are in jail at Tchollire-o!
Even those who are serving prison terms
At the Tchollire Prison-o!
Those at the Kondengui Robben Island,
Those who are chaffing in the
Nightmarish prison at Kondengui
Others are incarcerated at the Mantoum prison-o!
Others are jailed in Bamenda-o!
Not forgetting those in Buea jails!

Let me tell you this story.
I say let me narrate this tale to you.
A new national anthem has seen

The light of day in Ongola.
Some sort of national anthem
Has surfaced in Ongola.
In other words, a national anthem
Has been born in our land.
This is how our national anthem is chanted:

Cameroon is Cameroon,
So what can we do?
That is to say,
Cameroon is Cameroon,
What can we do?
In other words,
Cameroon na Cameroon,
What can we do?

Big Katika at Etoudi,
Has stolen all the money from State coffers,
We always sing:
Cameroon is Cameroon,
What can we do?
That is to say,
Cameroon is Cameroon,
What can we do?
In other words,
Cameroon na Cameroon,[10]
What shall we do about it?

Ministers embezzle State funds,
We sing nonstop:
Cameroon is Cameroon

---

[10] Cameroon is Cameroon

What shall we do now?
That is to say,
Cameroon is Cameroon
What can we do?
In other words,
Cameroon na Cameroon,
What can we do?

The Zangalewa batter
Students on strike on the campus
Of the University of Buea,
And even screw them,
We sing as usual:
Cameroon is Cameroon,
What are we going to do now?
That is to say,
Cameroon is Cameroon,
What can we do?
In other words
Cameroon na Cameroon
What can we do about it?

Mange-mille[11] kill taxi drivers
Because they have refused to choko[12],
We simply sing:
Camer is Camer,
So what can we do?
That is to say,
Cameroon is Cameroon,
What can we do?
In other words,

---

[11] Corrupt police officers
[12] Give bribes

A Cameroonian is a Cameroonian
What can we do about it?

Gendarmes rape bayam sellam[13]
Because they have refused to serve coffee[14]
We sing nonstop:
Cameroon is Cameroon,
What can we do about it?
That is to say,
Cameroon is Cameroon,
What can we do?
In other words,
Cameroon na Cameroon,
What can we do about it?

Politicians rig elections openly
Because they are afflicted
With megalomania,
We chante:
Ongola is Ongola,
What can we do about it?
That is to say,
Cameroon is Cameroon,
What can we do?
In other words,
Cameroon na Cameroon,
What can we do about it?

The ngomna refuses to put asphalt on the road,
Because ministers have stolen everything,
We sing shamelessly;

[13] Market women
[14] Give a bribe

53

Cameroon is Cameroon,
What can we do about it?
That is to say,
Cameroon is Cameroon
What can we do?
In other words,
Cameroon na Cameroon,
What can we do about it?

Civil servants are laid off
On account of economic crisis
And endemic corruption,
Due to systemic dysfunction,
We sing:
In ala word,
Cameroon na Cameroon,
We go do na how-no ?
Na so da we own
Hymne ongolais dei![15]

What can we do?
In other words,
Cameroon na Cameroon,
What can we do about it?
That's how we sing that
Camerian Anthem of ours!

University graduates

---

[15] That is to say,
Cameroon is Cameroon,
That's how we sing that
Cameroon National Anthem of ours!

Find themselves in Chomencam,
We sing like sheep:
Cameroon is Cameroon
What can we do about it?
That is to say,
Cameroon is Cameroon,
That's how we sing that
Cameroon National Anthem of ours!

Big Katika sadles us
With a constipated constitution
Because he wants to kick the bucket in office,
We sing stupidly,
Sheepishly I should say:
Cameroon is Cameroon
What can we do about it?
That is to say,
Cameroon is Cameroon,
That's how we sing that
Cameroon National Anthem of ours!

The Mbere-Khaki kill
Bendskin drivers because of nkap,
We sing:
Cameroon is Cameroon
What can we do about it?
That is to say,
Cameroon is Cameroon,
That's how we sing that
Cameroon National Anthem of ours!

Chop Pipo Dem Moni Party(CPDM)
Makes us see stars,

Because opposition political parties in Ongola
Cannot take up the gudgels,
 We sing like lunatics,
Cameroon is Cameroon
What can we do about it?
That is to say,
Cameroon is Cameroon,
That's how we sing that
Cameroon National Anthem of ours!

Big Katika withdraws every dime
From the Presidential Black Box
In order to go build his private
Hospital in Baden-Baden,
We sing timidly:
Cameroon is Cameroon
What can we do about it?
That is to say,
Cameroon is Cameroon,
That's how we sing that
Cameroon National Anthem of ours!

A wolowoss metamorphoses into First Lady,
We sing:
Cameroon is Cameroon
What can we do about it?
That is to say,
Cameroon is Cameroon,
That's how we sing that
Cameroon National Anthem of ours!

An Ongolan professor perplexed
By this state of affairs cries out:

Truly Cameroon is wonderful,
Let's live and let live,
That is to say:
Cameroon is a wonderful place
Let's keep watching,
It can't get any worse!

Excerpt from *Requiem pour Ongola en camfranglais: une poétique camerounaise* (2015), pp.1-3

Lorsque ce chep-ban de Mvomeka'a
Est come au kwat à Etoudi en 1982,
J'ai seulement langua aux capos que,
Mola, wuna lookot da djimtété.
Ils m'ont demandé que comment
Tu tok comme ça no mola?
Là là! J'ai mangé la terre en leur disant que:
Je nyè que ce mbenguiste qui est come au pouvoir
C'est un véritable come-no go.
Je leur ai tori que ce mola qu'on a chassé du séminaire
Pour je ne sais quelle raison,
Va quarrément foutre le Kamerun dans le caca!
Les tara ont refusé carrément de me ya,
Ils m'ont dit seulement que,
Djo, arrête de nous tchatcher come un djoun man
Y en a même qui m'ont dit de comot avec mon voum-là!
Autrement dit, il a m'ont pris pour
Un yoh qui ne leur fait que le sissia.
Je leur ai seulment montré mes
Attrapes–manioc en leur disant que
Mbombo, wuna cop nyè
Fais quoi, fais quoi vous allez nyè que

C'est moi qui tok le vrai toli,
Sep so ils m'ont dit de shut up!
Y en a même certains longs crayons
Qui ont komot leurs bics pour écrire
Des conneries que Godot
Est finalement arrivé à Ongola.
On a chanté, on a dansé à Yaounde à mort,
On a Soulé à Douala plenti,
On a nyoxé à Bafoussam comme des mabouls,
On a arrosé avec de l'odontol et du matango,
Tout ça, rien que pour célébrer l'arrivée au pouvoir
Du Roi-Fainéant camerounais.
Comme les Camers sont les vrais mboutoucous,
Nobody a nyè que le chop-chair
De Baba Toura est un bad diable!
Les journalistes de la CRTV ont même
Commencé leur one-man-show,
Ils ont chanté que Popaul est
Le nouveau Jacques Chirac ongolais
Certains radio-trottoirs sont allées
Jusqu'à toli everywhere que Paul Mbiaya
C'est le Messie que les Camers attendaient depuis from!
Beaucoup de pipo ont ont tok que
Paul Mbiaya c'est la manne divine
Qui est tombée du ciel sur la tête des Camers.
Les yoh et les yoyettes ont chanté et ont saka nonstop:
Popaul-eh! Popol-eh, notre cher président-eh!
Popaul-eh! Popol chaud gars-eh et patati et patata!
Nous voici au-day dans le zouazoua des chop-bluk-pot!
Vrai de Dieu, le Cameroun n'a rien à envier à Bagdad!
Ngola na Bagdad? Quelle guerre politique!
Tu go à Mamfe, na daso guerre partout!
Entre Agbor Tabi et Paul Ayah.

Ils sont à couteaux tirés nuit et jour.

Ngola no be na daso Bagdad?

Quelle guerre politique chez nous!

Les ennemis dans la maison-eh?

Tu go à Tiko, il y a le feu politique

Entre les autochtones et les grafis,

Guerre des sons of the soil contre

Les come-no-go originaires d'Abakwa.

Weh! Weh! Womohoh! On va faire comment?

Ngola est devenu Nagasaki and Hiroshima!

You go for Nkambe, na daso fire!

Il y a la guerre intestine entre

Awudu Mbaya Ibrahim et Shey Yembe Jones!

Bamenda dong ton be na Vietnam.

Tu go à Bamenda sep sep,

Il y a la guerre génocidaire entre

Les politiquarts assoifés de pouvoir.

Atanga and Angwafor say Fru Ndi must go for Baba

Ils veulent chasser le Chairman kaweh,

Dem say Chairman must rentrer dans son village natal.

Ngoketunjia don ton be na Waterloo!

Tu go à Ndop popo,

Il y a la guerre politique entre opposants et Rdpcistes.

Docta Lesigha and Fon Doh ne veulent pas nyè eye to eye

Popo me, I di askam say, hein:

C'est quand alors la fin de cette krish à Ongola?

Et la part de Popaul inside dis brouhaha?

No man no sabi. Allez donc dire si le peuple

A le droit de savoir la manière dont ils sont governés.

Les élus du peuple sont-ils là seulement pour faire

La politique du ventre au bled?

Autrement dire, sont-ils

Seulement les ventrologues?

59

Ou alors ils sont là seulement
Pour faire ami–ami avec leur idôle, Popol?
Je wanda seulement, hein.
How you sep you nyè dis affaire no mbombo?
Là où sommes-là, I see say il y a que les alamibous
Qui peuvent sortir les camers du ndoutou
Dans lequel ils s'enfoncent everyday…

English Translation

When this gang leader from Mvomeka'a
Came to Etoudi Quarter in 1982
I simply told my friends that,
Man, watch out for this djimtete.
They said to me:
Why are you talking like that, man?
Right there, I licked the ground and assured them that
This mbenguist who has come to power
Is a real come-no-go.
I added that this man who was sent away from the seminary
For reasons unknown to anyone
Is going to simply plunge Kamerun in deep shit.
My friends totally refused to listen to me;
They merely said I should stop talking like a drunk,
Some of them even said I should quit showing off!
In other words, they took me for
A bloke who was trying to intimidate them.
I simply show them my *attrapes-manioc*[16]
And told them:
Friends, you guys keep an eye on him

---

[16] teeth

No matter what, you'll agree with me one day that
My story is the right story.
Regardless, they told me to shut up!
Some long crayons even took out their pens
And started to write some inanities
That Godot has finally arrived in Ongola.
People sang, and danced in Yaounde like crazy
Folks drank themselves drunk in Douala,
People fucked in Bafoussam like dogs,
And drank odontol and matango,
All that simply to celebrate the accession to power
Of the Cameroonian *Roi-Fainéant*[17]
Given that Camerians are absolute mboutcoucous[18]
Nobody was able to figure out that the heir
Of Baba Toura is a bad devil!
Journalists at CRTV even started
Their own one-man-show,
They sang that Popaul is
The new Jacques Chirac of Ongola
Some radio-one-batteries even went
To the extent of saying that Paul Mbiaya
Is the Messiah that Camerians had
Been waiting for a long time ago!
Many people gossiped everywhere that
Paul Mbiaya is the manna that had fallen
From heaven onto the heads of Camerians.
Young boys and girls sang and danced nonstop:
Popaul-eh! Popol-eh! Our beloved president-eh!
Popaul-eh! Popol hot guy-eh and this and that!
Here we are today inside the zouzouaza of chop-bluk-pot!
I swear to God, Cameroon does not envy Bagdad!

---

[17] Lazy King
[18] Fools

Ngola is Bagdad? What a political battlefield!
You go to Mamfe, there's war everywhere!
Between Agbor Tabi and Paul Ayah.
They are at daggers drawn, day and night.
Ngola is simpy Bagdad?
Enemies in the house-eh!
You go to Tiko, there is political fire
Between indigenes and the grafi.
War between sons of the soil and
The come-no-go from Abakwa.
Weh! Weh! Womohoh! What can we do?
Ngola has become Nagasaki and Hiroshima!
You go to Nkambe, there's also fire!
There are internecine struggles between
Awudu Mbaya Ibrahim and Shey Yembe Jones!
Bamenda has become Vietnam.
You to Bamenda itself,
There is genocidal war
Between power-drunk political jugglers.
Atanga and Angwafor say Fru Ndi must return to Baba
They want to chase away Chairman once and for all.
They say Chairman must go back to his village of origin.
Ngoketunjia has become Waterloo!
You go to Ndop itself,
There is political war between members of
Opposition parties and CPDM party.
Docta Lesigha and Fon Doh don't
Want to see eye to eye.
I myself, hein, I am asking you this question:
When will this insane war come to an end in Ongola?
And Popaul's role in this brouhaha?
No one can say. So go figure if the populace
Has the right to know how they are being governed.

So the people's elected representatives are there
Simply to do politics of the stomach in this country?
To put this differently, are they simply belly politicians?
Or are they there simply to do buddy-buddy with their idol,
Popol?
I am only wandering, Hein.
Man, what's your take on this matter?
At the rate we are going
I think only witchdoctors
Will come get Camerians out of the ndoutou
In which they are getting buried everyday…

Chapter Five

Commentaries on the Translation Process

The translation of Fouda's text posed enormous problems on account of the pidginized nature of the French language she used in writing her story. Bandia (1997) defines pidgin as a "blend of African and European languages."(94-95) Two reasons account for Fouda's lexical choices in her novella. First, she wanted to employ the variety of French that is spoken by the youths in the major cities of Cameroon. Secondly, she was desirous of transposing Cameroonian linguistic and socio-cultural realities into her novel. Interestingly, this mode of writing is fast becoming the norm rather than the exception in postcolonial African fictional writing. As Bandia (1994) observes, "... for many of these writers this is a sure way of capturing the sociolinguistic and sociocultural realities of African life in the African novel."(93) Fouda's Camfranglais sentence structure is striking in that, although some French words are used, they are clearly patterned after Cameroonian oral discourse as seen in the following excerpt: "Midi, l'heure d'aller manger un peu, car votre estomac vous lance des insultes..." (10) We rendered this statement as: "It is midday; time to go find a little something to eat because your stomach is hauling insults at you." It should be noted that we translated "manger un peu" as "a little something to eat" because this is the manner in which Cameroonians talk among themselves in informal contexts. In a similar vein, the statement, "votre estomac vous lance des insultes" was translated literally as "your stomach is hauling insults at you", to provide local color. This rendition also made up for the lack of a target language equivalent that could capture the various shades of meaning implied by this expression.

Fouda tends to resort to neologisms in order to bridge cultural gaps between French and English as seen in the following excerpt: "Vous avez alors la possibilité d'aller manger au "tournedos". We translated this statement using the technique of calquing as follows: "So you have the opportunity to go eat at the "tournedos." Jones (1997) notes that "a linguistic calque is a…copy of an original. It is a translated borrowing: the borrowing of a foreign word or group of words by literal translation of its components. (53) The reason we simply transposed the source-text lexeme "tournedos" into the target text is that the socio-cultural reality harbored by the word 'tournedos" does not exist in the target-text community. There is no standard French equivalent of "tournedos "because this social reality does not exist in France. Tournedos is a social reality specific to Cameroon. To disambiguate the semantic connotation of the utterance, we provided an explicatory note in the glossary section of this book: makeshift restaurant; roadside restaurant; turn-back restaurant.

Another neologism that necessitated an interpretive reading of Fouda's text for the purpose of translation is the word "mamie" as in "mamie koki" , "mamie ndolè" , "mamie atchomo"(10). The difficulty of translating these expressions stems from the fact that "mamie" is a polysemous word endowed with several significations. The word "mamie" is the Pidgin equivalent of the standard French word "mère" (mother). Cameroonian youths generally address older women as "mamie" as a sign of respect for persons of a certain age. However, in the business arena, the word is used as an epithet for a woman who specializes in the cooking of specific kinds of food for commercial purposes. Furthermore, in a filial relationship, "mamie" would be used to address one's mother.

We provided an explanatory note in the glossary to shed light on the contextual usage of the word "mamie": elderly woman, business woman of a certain age.

Fouda's style of writing raises questions about the nature of the French she uses to communicate her thought pattern and imagination. Her French is neither Pidginized nor standard French. The French she uses is a variety that tends to get closer and closer to African vernaculars (Bandia, 1994, p.100) as the following excerpt shows: "Mamie, fais-moi le 'beau-regard' ou 'l'oiseau.'"(11) A translator who is not familiar with Cameroonian francanglais would have a hard time deciphering the signigications embedded in this utterance. Resorting to the literal translation technique would obscure the communicative intent and would result in nonsensical rendition such as the following: "Mamie, serve me the good-looks and the bird." This sort of translation would break down communication completely. Yet, Fouda's recourse to Camfranglais enhances the Africanness of her writing and brings into the limelight the setting in which her novel is conceived. In our translation, we rendered it as "Mamie, serve me the good-looks and the bird." However, in the glossary found at the end of this book we have provided an interpretation of these two expressions after carefully studying the contextual clues provided by Fouda herself. This paratextual material is indispensable for readers who are not fluent speakers of Camfranglais. We did this because it is important for the translator to retain those textual aspects that account for the indigenous aspects of the work. Agreeing with us on this point is Berman (1985) who contends that "L'effacement des vernaculaires est… une grave atteinte à la textualité des oeuvres en prose."(79)[The effacement of vernaculars … is a serious infringement on the textuality of prose.] We have opted to retain Fouda's *Camerounismes*[19] in our translation because it is important to represent society in a novel holistically by transposing sociolinguistic factors that fully capture the background of the characters as seen in the following statement: "Ma soeur, tu lui as fait 'Annaba'."(13) This soccer imagery is so important for discourses in a soccer-loving nation such as Cameroon that mistranslating it would be tantamount to defacing the socio-cultural information that the writer intended to convey. In the translation we retained the word "Annaba but provided an elucidation in the glossary: "Waterloo of the Indomitable Lions."

Je parle camerounais: pour un renouveau franfaune is challenging for the literary translator in many respects but the thorniest problem that complicated our translation project was the writer's constant recourse to semantic shifts as a narrative trope as is evident in the following excerpt: "Au tournedos, officie l' "asso". L'"asso", diminutif flatteur de "associé(e), est cette personne chez qui vous faites régulièrement des achats et qui, lorsque c'est "fort sur vous", vous fait "manger un credit…."(10) This statement is an indication that in Fouda's writing orality and the written word are in a continuum. Writing along similar lines, Obiechina observes that in African fictional writing, a synthesis takes place in which characteristics of the oral culture survive and are absorbed, assimilated, extended, and even re-organized within a new cultural experience. Also vital aspects of the oral literature are absorbed into an emerging written literature of greatly invigorated forms infused with vernacular energy through metaphors, images and symbols, more complex plots, and diversified structures of meaning.("Narrative Proverbs in the African Novel", 123) Fouda makes a conscious effort to keep both oral and written

---

[19] Cameroonian turns of phrase

communication forms in cohesion in her narrative. In the example above, there are close ties between the oral and the written word. Oral tradition cannot be dissociated from her text because, like her counterparts in Africa, she is steeped in the indigenous cultures of her people and tends to make use of oral motifs and images in her literary creativity. Consequently,

we rendered the statement as "eat a credit" for the reasons provided above. However, a footnote, generally referred to as 'translator's note' was added: "pay for your meal later" to shed light on this seemingly nonsensical statement.

Some of the constructions that we struggled with in the course of translating the excerpt from Fouda's text are those that were charged with significations revealing a great deal about the worldview and imagination of the characters as seen in the following extract:

Le jazz est cette légumineuse de nom commun "haricot", musicalement appellée ainsi parce l'ingestion de ce protoide azoté provoque chez le consommateur des fuites sonores ressemblant à s'y méprendre au son d'une trompette." Lorsque les haricots sont recouverts d'huile, on les qualifie de "jazz sous-marin. (9)

This passage harbors a lot of information about the culinary habits as well as the vocabulary that goes with the feeding habits of Cameroonians. Fouda's lexical choices are likely to throw off the translator who is unacquainted with the worldview of Camfranglophones. At first sight, the correlation between a trumphet, a musical instrument, and beans, a food item, seems far-fetched. More confusion is created when

Fouda resorts to a semantic shift that tranforms beans into submarines!

We surmounted these hurdles by calquing the source text statements in the target text and providing elucidatory notes in the glossary. However, it is worth noting that our translation into standard English in the glossary does not carry the same weight as the orginal French text because the speech peculiarity of the Camfranglais speaker is lost in the translation process. There is something missing in the translation; something we would like to refer to as the "cameroonianness" of the communication. A more faithful rendition of the excerpt could be achieved by rendering both the content and the form of the utterance which are grounded in the sociocultural setting of Cameroonian society. Nonetheless, the translator's effort is commendable. It would require just a little stretch of the imagination on the part of the reader to grasp the holistic message in the target text.

Vakunta's two texts pose thorny translation problems. One such problem is how to deal with words that exist in Camfranglais and sound French but are non-existent in standard French language. In "Hymne camerien", for instance, we struggled with the translation of "Les sauveteurs du Mbanga-o!" Part of the problem is attributable to the fact the word "sauveteur" is a *camerounisme* coined from the French expression *vendeur à la sauvette* (hawker, peddler). Translating this word as "vendeur à la sauvette" would deprive the text of its socio-cultural praxis because the practice of the *vendeur à la sauvette* is European—specifically French. Translation practice involves transition from one linguistic culture into an alien linguistic culture. It is in this respect that Bandia (1993) posits that "translation is an intercultural activity as well as an intralingual one as it deals with (at least) two linguistic systems embedded in two different cultures."(55) Cognisant of this truism, we rendered the statement as "The sauveteurs in Mbanga-o!" We then provided a translator's note in the glossary to enable the monolingual reader of the target text to get a rough idea of the signification of the source-text signifier. It has been noted by Snell-Hornby (1988) that the "extent to which a text is translatable varies with the degree to which it is embedded in its own specific culture, also with the cultural background of the source text and target audience in terms of time and place."(41) In the excerpt above, we have endeavored to preserve the sociocultural content of the source language. This observation leads us to the conclusion according to which the translation process defies the traditional approach which views translation as a mere substitution of linguistic and cultural equivalents (Bandia, 1993).

Another perplexing problem that we had to surmount in the translation of "Hymne camerien" is the poet's predilection for code-mixing as seen in this extract:

> Laissez-moi vous langua cette nouvelle.
> I sei mek I langua wuna dis tori.
> Un nouvel hymne national vient de naître à Ongola.
> Some national anthem dong commot for Ongola. (57)

In this excerpt alone, three different codes have been employed interchangeably by the poet to convey the same message. The first verse is a mix of standard French (laissez-moi vous... cette nouvelle) and Duala (langua). The second verse is a hybrid code born out of Pidgin English (I sei mek... wuna dis tori) and Duala (langua). The third verse is written entirely in Standard French, and the fourth verse is written entirely in Cameroon Pidgin English. This code-mixing could be the bane of a literary translator tasked with looking for an appropriate translation model that does justice to the source text message as well as the form of the target language. To achieve a faithful translation, the translator has to ensure that meaning and form are inseparable. In other words, the translator would be better off adopting a translation paradigm that ties the semantic content of the source text to the form of the target text. Concurring with us is Peter Newmark (1981) who observes that "semantic translation attempts to recreate the tone and flavor and elegance of the original and in this process, words are sacred not because they are more important than the content, but because form and content are one.(47) With all this in mind, we rendered the above-mentioned excerpt as follows:

> Let me tell you this story.
> I say let me narrate this story to you.
> A new national anthem has seen the light of day in Ongola.
> Some sort of national anthem has surfaced in Ongola.

The additional explanatory notes we provided in the glossary in a bid to provide the target-text reader with supplementary information is the right thing to do in the mind of Newmark who notes that, if the SL text is entirely bound up with the culture of the SL community—a novel or a historical piece or a description attempting to characterize a place or custom of local character—the translator has to decide whether or not the reader requires, or is entitled to, supplementary information and explanation(1981, p.21)

We have endeavored in the course of our translation to preserve the Cameroonian thought pattern and worldview by infusing the European language with Cameroonian sociocultural specificities. One such sociocultural reality is reference to "Chomencam" in the statement:

Les diplômés d'université
Se retrouvent au Chomencam
On chante comme des moutons;
Le Cameroun c'est le Cameroun (61),
 which we rendered as:
University graduates
Find themselves in Chomencam,
We sing like sheep:
Cameroon is Cameroon

It is worth noting that with regard to the rendition of the word 'Chomencam' (endemic unemployment in Cameroon); we resorted to the loan translation technique because rendering it simply as 'unemployment' would divest the source language word of this contextual signification, thus resulting in under-translation. Under-translation refers to the situation where the information contained in the target language is less than that of the source language. We deemed it necessary to retain this cultural specificity because "translation is transference of culture", to paraphrase Mian Wang (2012, p.129).

Recourse to pidginization as a narrative trope posed some translation problems as seen in the following excerpt:

In ala word,
Cameroon na Cameroon,
We go do na how-no ?
Na so da we own
Hymne ongolais dei! (61)
This stanza is written entirely in Cameroon Pidgin English.
And we have rendered it in English as follows:
In ala word,
Cameroon na Cameroon,

We go do na how-no?
Na so da we own
Hymne ongolais dei!

We realize that rendering this stanza in standard English would be problematic for two reasons. First, African writers generally opt for pidginized forms of European languages in order to illustrate the classic case of what happens when two or more alien languages come into contact. Second, authors resort to pidginization as a medium of fictional writing because they want to shed light on aspects of communication in speech communities characterized by polyglossia. It is for these reasons that Bandia (1994) notes that "West Africans use pidgin in their verbal interaction with uneducated West Africans from different ethnic groups, also to talk among themselves in certain informal contexts."(94) He further observes that West Africans of all backgrounds use pidgin as a means of ensuring group solidarity, and reinforcing a sense of integration. This is the use of language which Malinowski refers to as phatic communion (Bandia, 1994, p.94).

In the light of the foregoing, we resorted to *borrowing* as a translation paradigm and provided a footnote to shed light on the meaning of the source text. According to Jones (1997) a linguistic borrowing is "a translation device born of a deficiency in the T.L."(41). It should be noted that in our case, our choice is not determined by T.L. linguistic deficiency; rather it is the need to preserve the communicative intent of the source text that accounted for our choice. This goes to show that in order to produce a balanced translation of a text written in Camfranglais, the translator has to steer clear of the temptation to rely on the technique of merely substituting linguistic elements in the source text with equivalent linguistic elements in the target language as suggested by Catford (1965).

In addition to expressing African thought in a European language, the translator also has to deal with the unique problem posed by the non-standardized forms of European languages, namely, pidgin, creoles and more. Translation transpires between two languages but as every seasoned translator would acknowledge, language is a carrier of culture. In this light, Wang (2012) notes that "translation activity is essentially meant to graft information from the source language culture to the target language culture."(131) It is this approach that we adopted in our translation of "Hymne camerien".

Our translation of the excerpt from Requiem *pour Ongola en Camfranglais; une poétique camerounaise* (2015) was far from seamless. Translation problems cropped up at the level of the poet's lexical choices that harbored formidable comprehension challenges as seen in the following verses: " Lorsque ce chep-ban de Mvomeka'a/Est come au quat à Etoudi en 1982/ J'ai seulement langua aux capos que.../(1). Interestingly, this sort of linguistic hybridization seems to be the poet's style of preference. However, this mode of writing is rife with translation hurdles. The word "chep-ban", for instance, is a deconstruction of sorts of the standard French statement: "chef des bandits." This indigenization of Metropolitan French by the poet tends to obfuscate meaning for the source text reader who may not necessarily be familiar with the etymology of this camfranglais coinage. By resorting to the domestication of French the poet gives prominence to the kind of informal French that is spoken by Cameroonian youths who perceive recourse to franglais as an identity and group solidarity marker. In this regard, Fonkoua (2015) observes that "One of the main functions of Camfranglais is as a youth identity language... It is used in different peer-groups as a marker of in-group belonging and solidarity. As an identity marker, it is also used to indicate belonging to urban youth and modernity."(29)

In the translation process, we relied partially on context clues, the most helpful of which are "Mvomeka'a" and "Etoudi". The two words used together in this poem leads the savvy translator to infer that the poet is making reference to the Cameroonian Head of State, whose notoriety for wheeling and dealing with men of the underworld is an open secret in Cameroon. It should be noted, though, that contextual clues may not be enough to get the translator out of discursive conundrum. Knowledge of the political culture of Cameroon is of great necessity for a faithful rendition of this excerpt, which we did as follows: When this gang leader from Mvomeka'a /Came to Etoudi Quarter in 1982/I simply told my friends that…/

It is worth noting that we have capitalized the word 'Quarter' in 'Etourdi Quarter' in order to allude to the Presidential Palace at Etoudi in Yaounde. This may look like a deviation from the source-text formalistic norm but the need to elucidate warrants this sort of deviation, if deviation it is. Other lexical choices that slowed down the translation process are words such as mbenguiste (someone who travels to Europe); tchatcher(to chat; chat up a girl); voum (bragging); djoun (drunk); longs crayons(intellectuals); feymania (swindling); feyman(con man); feywoman (con woman); zouazoua (illicit fuel smuggled from Nigeria into Cameroon).

All too often, the poet resorts to the lexical formative process of compounding as seen in "Je leur ai seulement montre mes/ Attrapes-manioc en leur disant que…/ (1) Les "attrape-manioc" is a reference to human teeth. Because the staple food of the people that the poet is alluding to is cassava (manioc) he uses this compound word in reference to teeth. 'Attraper le manioc' avec ses dents is to 'eat a meal of

76

cassava'. This usage clearly shows that the French in Vakunta's text has been subjected to indigenization (or domestication)in order to reflect Cameroonian socio-cultural realities. The linguistic manipulation that takes place in this poem is indicative of the poet's conscious effort to translate orality into the written word; to fuse oral traditions with the print culture for the purpose of expressing a unique worldview, cultural specificity and self-identity.

Another compound word that defies translation in this excerpt is 'chop-bluk-pot' as seen in the following extract: "Nous voici auday dans le zouazoua des chop-bluk-pot!"(2) which we rendered as: "Here we are today inside the zouazoua of chop-bluk-pot!" It is noteworthy that we resorted to the calque technique by retaining the source-text lexeme 'chop-bluk-pot' in the target text in a bid to retain the source-text aesthetics and cultural semantics. After all, translation is an activity that entails the transfer of culture: As Papastergiadis (2000) observes, "We have come to appreciate that cultures do not need to be rooted in a given place, that fragments of culture can survive in multiple places, that cultural meanings may leap across generations and transform themselves across the gaps of time."(123). Papastergiadis then goes on to shed light on the concept of translation as a metaphor for understanding how the foreign and the familiar are interrelated in every form of cultural production. Writing along similar lines, Bandia (1993) notes that "cultural value systems are difficult to grasp as they are intricately woven in the texture of the native language. A conscious translator, therefore, must be willing to make the extra effort that is required to unearth the full cultural meaning hidden in the language."(56) 'Chop-bluk-pot' is a pidginized expression derived from three English language words: eat, break and pot. It is a derogatory expression often used by Cameroonians to describe someone who lives from day to day and does not bother to save for a rainy day. The usage of this word has garnered political undertones over time in the sense that Cameroonians generally employ it as a lampoon on the Beti, the ethnic group from which the Cameroonian Head of State hails. Most Cameroonians perceive this group as being responsible for the economic doldrums that have plagued Cameroon from 1982 (year of President Paul Biya's accession to power) to date.

Onomastics, the art of naming, is an aspect of Vakunta's poetry that we found challenging in the translation process. Many reasons account for this difficulty but the most cogent explanation is the fact that in most African cultures, virtually every name has a context. As Robert Miller and Gloria Onyeoziri (2014) have noted, "The contextual significance of these names implies that each of them is the product of some experience, which produces a creative exercise that gives rise to the name" ("Ironic Onomastic Strategies..." 83). These writers further observe that if names carry meaning, they are also open to the charge of irony. It is this quest for fictive irony that spurred Vakunta to resort to names such as "Mbiaya" (2), "Popol" (2), "Baba Toura" (2), and "Chairman" (3). When the poet writes: "Paul Mbiya c'est la manne divine/Qui est tombée du ciel sur la tête des Camers" (2), informed writers reading his poem can sense the ironic undertones with which the poet intended to load his versification. In fact, most Cameroonians view their Head of State as a public liability; not manna from heaven. One element of nomenclature that lends credibility to the poet's suggestive contradiction is the deformation of President Paul Biya's family name. By rebaptizing the president 'Mbiaya', the poet's achieves more than just satire. He actually succeeds in thingifying the Head of State by toying with his name.In the translation process; we refrained from tampering with the morphology of these names because we perceive them as cultural repositories within the framework of literature. Arguing with us along similar lines is Gabrielle Schwab (2012) who posits that "Literature is a medium that writes culture within the particular space and mode of aesthetic production. It therefore uses discursive and figurative modes, regimes of knowledge, and structures of appeal that are specific to literature and related aesthetic practices."(2) Rather than attempt a re-naming we provided a glossary at the end of our translation in order to shed ample light on the contextual signification of the poet's onomastic choices. In the absence of a glossary, we would strongly recommend the insertion of a translator's note that fulfills the function of illumination.

The same holds true for the rendition of the name 'Baba Toura' in the following verse: "Baba Toura est un bad diable."(2)It should be noted that 'Baba Toura' is a sobriquet for the erstwhile Cameroon Head of State, Ahmadou Ahidjo, for whom most Cameroonians had an aversion on account of his iron-fisted style of ruling the country for over two decades as evidenced by the poet's recourse to qualifiers such as 'diable'[devil]and 'bad' in the excerpt above. To be a devil is bad enough but to be a "bad devil is even worse. Thus, The name 'Baba Toura' is reflective of the impersonable nature of the person it represents. The overall effect of the insertion of this name in Camfranglais literature is one of subversive and satirical representation of the social, historical and political worldview of Camanglophones. In our rendition of the aforementioned verse, we kept "Baba Toura' in a bid to avoid doing damage to the socio-cultural import of the poet's lexical choice. Mindful of the importance of background information in the translation process, we provided an explicatory note in the glossary.

Our attempts at translating the word 'chairman' resuscitated the phantoms of untranslatability, the more so

79

because 'chairman' is a polysemous lexeme. Polysemy lends itself to multiple interpretations. Merriam-Webster's Collegiate Dictionary (Tenth Edition, 2001) defines the term 'chairman' as: "the presiding officer of a meeting or an organization or committee; the administrative officer of a department of instruction, as in college."(188) However, it is interesting to note that in the Cameroonian context which Vakunta's poem references, the term 'chairman' refers not only to the leader of a political party but particularly to the leader of the oppositional Social Democratic Front (SDF)Party. The SDF party leader is called Ni John Fru Ndi. It ensues from this notation that in the Cameroonian context names harbor both generic and specific significations. This is even truer in the realm of creative writing. Arguing along the same lines, Bill F. Ndi (2014) posits: Names and naming are an important ingredient in the creative tradition of the new and emerging literature of the Cameroons and have found sanctuary in the literary landscape of authors from the English-speaking Cameroons specifically ("The Global Reader and Names…" 123)

Ndi then goes on to pose a question which is deemed of great import to this study: "Do ACL writers in poetizing names follow any convention be it informally or internationally agreed upon?"(124) In the response to his own question, Ndi notes that in Anglophone literature names are used by the literary artist as a guiding philosophy for a people's history and their place in a globalizing world. In other words, names have the potential to provide information that would otherwise remain concealed were the reader to learn nothing of the intercultural blending that accompanies the act of naming. Vakunta's transposition of the name 'chairman' into his poetry opens a floodgate of socio-cultural as well as political interpretations. The term 'chairman' is not just a sobriquet for Ni John Fru

Ndi, leader of the Social Democratic Party, but it also symbolizes an historical event; the birth of the first post-independence oppositional political party in Cameroon as well as the advent of political pluralism in this nation-state. From the philosophical perspective, 'chairman' carries in its wake undertones of a new dispensation in Cameroon—multiparty politics. As can be seen from the foregoing discourse, the generic connotation of the word 'chairman' has acquired other significations as seen in this verse: "Il veulent chasser le Chairman kaweh"(3), which we rendered as: "They want to chase away Chairman once and for all." It is noteworthy that this translation does not fully transpose the linguistic richness of the source text into the target text. The source text is written in three languages—French, English and Hausa. On the other hand, the target text is a monolingual text written in standard English. Cognisant of this under-translation, we provided a note in the glossary in a bid to shed more light. The innumerable bottle-necks we encountered in the translation of the corpus above lend credence to the assertion by Walter Benjamin (1968) according to which poetry as a literary genre tends to defy the art of translation. In other words, translation is, more or less, a provisional way of coming to terms with the foreignness of languages.

Chapter Six

Conclusion

The intent of this book has not been simply to provide readers with information on the plethora of modes of writing Camfranglais literature. The purport has been to aid translators of Camfranglais literature, in their reflections on the nature of texts they are called upon to translate for different readerships, and propose paradigms suitable for translating such literature. The question that begs to be asked at this juncture is why it is critical for translators of Camfranglais literature to be conversant with evolutionary trends inherent in the theory and practice of translating such literature. We maintain that mastery of French language alone does not suffice to do justice to the translation of the novels discussed in this book. Translators of Camfranglais literature cannot but be like the texts they translate—at once multilingual and multicultural. Given the polytonality, Polyvocality, cross-cultural and multilingual composition of Camfranglais literary texts, translators must conceive models suitable for translating these texts. The texts analyzed in this book irrefutably call for multidimensional frameworks for translation if the end-product must pass the text of textual reliability. Robinson (2012) defines 'textual reliability as follows:

> A text's reliability consists in the trust a user can place in it, or encourage others to place in it, as a representation or reproduction of the original. To put that differently, a text's reliability consists in the user's willingness to base future actions on an assumed relation between the original and the translation (7)

It is clear from this definition that the reliability of a translated text resides principally in the end users' belief that the translation gives them the kind of information they need about the original that a course of action will not abort as a result of the translation. Our commentaries on the translated extracts discussed above lead to the conclusion that the translation of Camfranglais literature defies recourse to paradigms that have stood the test of time by meeting the needs of translators of metropolitan French literature. These models are not suitable for the translation of peripheral literatures written in less commonly taught languages such as Camfranglais because the texts are ethnographic and culture-oriented. The texts we translated above in a bid to validate our proposed model make the translation process buckle due to the multiple articulations of Frenchness in these texts. Yet, we achieved laudable success in the rendition process by having recourse to paratextual contraptions.

The Hermeneutic–Exegetic Model proposed in this book serves as an efficacious antidote to the translation 'ailments' diagnosed during our translation of the corpus above. Three reasons account for the effectiveness of the model as a canon for the translation of works written in Camfranglais. First, it is a multidimensional paradigm that carters to the plurivocality of the texts that come out of French-speaking Cameroon. Second, it is a two-pronged framework that creates an interface between the textual and non-textual constituents of the text intended for translation. This constitutive binarism does not make the task of the translator any easier. What it does is that it enables the translator to position himself or herself on the formalistic and substantive borders of the literary text in a bid to unravel the linguistic and extralinguisitc factors that account for textual holism. Last but not least, the Hermeneutic-Exegetic model lends itself to usage in conjunction with the

Bloomian taxonomic model of literary analysis which has proven to be effective in de-problematizing translation practice. Though conceived to serve the needs of pedagogues, the Bloomian Taxonomy, named after Benjamin Bloom (1956) is applicable to translation studies. It is a critical analytic model that enables the reader of a source text to detect not just the non-verbal communication cues in written texts but also the situational attributes that constitute the matrix of the author's creative genius.

Language, whether it is considered from its etymological standpoint or from the perspective of the problems created by the translation of socio-cultural reality into a hegemonic language that did not shape that reality and was not shaped by it, remains one of the intractable aspects of translating the texts we have examined in this book. This gray area, undoubtedly, leaves room for further investigation. Avenues for further research include the implementation of the framework proposed in this book in the translation of works written in other African creoles and pidgins. In particular, it would be interesting to attempt a wide application of our model to the translation of literature written in Ivorian *Nouchi*, Kenyan *Sheng*, Senegalese *Franlof*, Congolese *Lingala*, South African *Tsotsitaal* and Centrafrican *Fransango*. A study of the translations of African literary works written entirely in Pidgin English such as Ken Saro-Wiwa's *SozaBoy* (1995) would be illuminating. Like Cameroonians, these writers view themselves to be at the 'crossroads 'of languages. Their texts are emblematic of the linguistic ambivalence that constitutes the life-blood of social intercourse in the communities in which the works are written.

It is evident from the critical analysis we have done in the preceding pages that the indigenization of the ex-colonizer's language in the writing process by the previously colonized poses enormous problems for the literary translator, and invites new modes of reading and translation. In his introduction to the translation of Martin Buber's *I and Thou* (1970),Kaufmann observes that readers need to feel addressed by the books they read, as if the writer were speaking directly to them. This certainly holds true for the translator of Camfranglais literature as well, the moreso because "le text tel qu'il est écrit aujourd'hui en espace francophone est une traversée des langues et une interrogation sur la fonction du langage" (Gauvin, 1997, p.14) [the text such as it is written today in the Francophone zone is a mosaic of languages and an interrogation of the function of language.]

Works cited

Ashcroft, Bill, Gareth Griffiths, Helen Tiffin. Eds. *The Empire Writes Back: Theory and Practice in Post-colonial Literatures*. London and New York: Routledge, 1989.

Bandia, Paul. "Translation as Culture Transfer: Evidence from African Creative Writing." *Traduction, Terminologie, Rédaction* 6.2. (1993), 55-78.

_____. "On Translating Pidgins and Creoles in African Literature." *Traduction, Terminologie, Rédaction* 7.2(1993), 94-114.

Benjamin, Walter. "The Task of the Translator: An Introduction to the Translation of Baudelaire's *Tableaux Parisiens*." *Illuminations*. Trans. Harry Zohn. Ed. Hanna Arendt.New York: Harcourt, Brace & World, Inc., 1968; 69-82.

Berman, A. *Les Tours de Babel: essai sur la traduction*. Mauvezin: Trans-Europ, 1985.

Biloa, Edmond. *La Langue française au Cameroun: analyse linguistique et didactique.*New York: Peter Lang, 2004.

_____. *Le français en contact avec l'anglais au Cameroun*. Munchen: LINCOM Europa, 2006.

Bissaya-Bessaya, Euloge Thierry. *Le Camfranglais*. Saint Denis: Edilivre, 2014.

Bloom. S.Benjamin. *Taxonomy of Educational Objectives*. New York: David McKay, 1956.

Buber, Martin. *I and Thou*. Trans. Walter Kaufmann. New York: Simon and Schuster, 1970.

Catford, J.C. A *Linguistic Theory of Translation*. Oxford: Oxford University Press, 1965.

Derrida, Jacques. "Des Tours de Babel." *Difference in Translation*.Ed.and Trans. Joseph F. Graham. Ithaca: Cornell UP, 1985.165-207

Echu, George. "Influence of Cameroon Pidgin English on the Cultural Development of the French Language" (1991). Retrieved on March 12, 2014 from https://www.indiana.edu/~iulcwp/pdfs/03-echu03.pdf
_____. "Pidginization of French in Cameroon" (2006). Retrieved on February 12, 2014 from http://www.inst.at/trans/16Nr/01_5/echu16.htm

Eco, Umberto. *Experiences in Translation*. Toronto: University of Toronto press, 2001.

Ferral, Carole de. *Le Pigin-english du Cameroun*. Paris: Peters/ SELAF, 1989.
_____. "Décrire un parler jeune: le Camfranglais (Cameroun) in *français en Afrique* (*Revue du Reseau des Observations du Français Contemporain en Afrique*), No.21, Nice, Institut de Linguistique française- CNRS, UMR6039, pp.257-265.

Fonkou K. Gabriel. *Moi taximan*. Paris: L'Harmattan, 2001.

Fonkoua, H. Kamdem. *A Dictionary of Camfranglais*. Frankfurt am Main: Peter Lang, 2015.

Fouda, Mercédès. *Je parle camerounais: pour un renouveau francofaune*.Paris: Karthala, 2001.

Gauvin, Lise. *L'écrivain francophone à la croisée des langues*. Paris: Editions Karthala, 1997.

Gyasi, Kwaku, A. "Writing as Translation: African Literature and the Challenges of Translation." Research *in African Literatures* 30.2 (1999): 75-87.
_____."The African Writer as a Translator: Writing African Languages through French." *Journal of African studies* 16.2(2003):143-159.

_____. *The Francophone African Text: Translation and the Postcolonial Experience*. Frankfurt am Main: Peter Lang, 2006.

Jameson, Frederic. "Third-World Literature in the Era of Multinational Capitalism." *Social Test* 5.3 (1986):65-88.

Jones, H. Michelle. *The Beginning Translator's Handbook, Or the ABCs of French-English Translation*. New York: UPA, 2014.

Khatibi, Abelkebir. *Amour bilingue. Montpellier: Fata Morgana, 1983*.

Kouega, Paul. 2003. "Camfranglais: A novel slang in Cameroon schools." *English Today* 19.2, 23-29.

_____. Kouega, Jean-Paul. Camfranglais: *A Glossary of Common Words, Phrases and Usages*. Muenchem: LINCOM EUROPA, 2013.

Kubler, George. *The Shape of Time: Remarks on the History of Things*. New Haven: Yale University Press, 1962.

Magot, Jean Claude. "Exegesis and Translation." Retrieved January 10, 2016 from http://biblicalstudies.org.uk/pdf/eq/1978-3_156.pdf

Mendo Zé, Gervais. *Le français langue africaine: Enjeux et atouts pour la Francophonie*. Paris: Publisud, 1999.

Miller, Robert and Gloria Onyeoziri. «Ironic Onomastic Strategies of Calixte Beyala and Chimamanda Adichie.» Eds. Adaku T. Ankumah. *Nomenclatural Poetization and Globalization*.Bamenda:Langaa Research & Publishing, CIG, 2014.

Ndi, F. Bill. «The Global Reader and Names in Literary Works by Peter W. Vakunta, Bill F.Ndi and Emmanuel Fru Doh. » Eds. Adaku T. Ankumah. *Nomenclatural Poetization and Globalization*.Bamenda:Langaa Research & Publishing, CIG, 2014.

Newmark, Peter. *Approaches to Translation*. Oxford: Pergamon Press, 1981.

Nganang, Patrice. *Temps de chien : chronique animale*. Paris: Serpent à Plumes, 2001.

_____. *Dog Days*. Trans. Amy Baram Reid. Charlottesville: University of Virginia Press, 2001.

Ntsobé, André-Marie, George Achu, Edmond Biloa. eds. *Le camfranglais, quelle parlure? Etude linguistique et sociolinguistique*. Frankfurt am Main: Peter Lang, 2008.

Obiechina, Emmanuel. "Narrative Proverbs in the African novel." *Research in African Literatures* 24.4 (1993): 123-140.

_____."Transition from Oral to Literary Tradition." Présence Africaine 63.3 (1967): 140-161.

_____. "Problem of Language in African Writing: The Example of the Novel." *The Conch* 5.1-2(1973): 11-28.

_____. *Culture, Tradition and Society in the West African Novel*. Cambridge: Cambridge University Press, 1975.

_____. *Language and Theme: Essays on African Literature*. Washington D.C.: Howard Universtity Press, 1990.

Ojo-Ade, Femi. "The Role of the Translator of African Literature in Intercultural Consciousness and Relationships"*Meta* 31.3 (1986):291-299.

_____."The Literary Translator, Messenger or Murderer? A Study of Oyono's *Une vie de boy* and Reed's *Houseboy*." Ed. Femi Ojo-Ade. *On Black Culture*. Ile-Ife: Obafemi Awolowo University Press, 1989.

Omole, James O. "Code-switching in Soyinka's *The Interpreters*." Eds. Epstein, L. Edmund and Robert Kole. *The Language of African Literature*.Trenton: Africa World Press, 1998.

Papastergiadis, Nikos. *The Turbulence of Migration: Globalization, Deterritorialization and Hybridity*. Cambridge: Polity Press, 2000.

Quayson, Ato. *Post-colonialism: Theory, Practice or Process?* Cambridge: Polity Press, 2000.

Riccardi, Alessandra. *Translation Studies: Perspectives on an Emerging Discipline*. Cambridge: Cambridge University Press, 2002.

Robinson, Douglas. *Becoming a Translator: An Introduction to the Theory and Practice of Translation*. London & New York: Routledge, 2012.

Saro-Wiwa, Ken. *Sozaboy: A Novel in Rotten English*. London: Longman African Writers Series, 1994.

Schleiermacher, Friedrich. "On the Different Methods of Translation." In Translation and Literature 4.1 (1995), 5-30.

Snell-Hornby, M. *Translation Studies: An Integrated Approach*. Amsterdam: 1988.

Steiner, George. *After Babel: Aspects of Language and Translation*. New York: Oxford University Press, 1975.

Schwab, Gabrielle. *Imaginary Ethnographies: Literature, Culture and Subjectivity*. New York: Columbia University Press, 2012

Tervonen, Taina. "L'écrivain à l'école de la rue. Entretien avec Patrice Nganang," *Africulture*, No. 37, 2001.

Tonkin, Humphrey and Maria Esposito Frank. *The Translator as Mediator of Cultures*. Philadelphia: John Benjamins Publishing Company, 2010.

Vakunta, Wuteh P. *Indigenization in the African Francophone Novel: A New Literary Canon*. Frankfurt am Main: Peter Lang, 2011.

_____. *Camfranglais: The Making of a New Language in Cameroonian Literature*. Bamenda: Langaa Research and Publishing, 2014

_____. On Translating Camfranglais and Other Camerounismes." *Meta* 53.4(2008):942-947.

_____. *Speak Camfranglais pour un renouveau ongolais.* Bamenda: Langaa Research and Publishing CIG, 2014.

_____. *Requiem pour Ongola en Camfranglais: Une poétique camerounaise.* Bamenda: Langaa Research and Publishing CIG, 2015.

Venuti, Lawrence. *The Translator's Invisibility: A History of Translation.* New York & London: Routledge, 1995.

Vinay, J.P. et J.Darbelnet. *Stylistique compare du français et de l'anglais: méthode de traduction.Paris: Didier, 1958.*

Webster, Merriam. *Merriam Webster' Collegiate Dictionary* (10th edition): Springfield: Merriam-Webster, Incorporated, 2001.

Wang, Mian. "An Analysis of Over-translation and Under-translation in Perspective of Cultural Connotation." *Lecture Notes in Information Technology,* 16-17(2012): 129-133.

Zabus, Chantal. *The African Palimpsest: Indigenization of Language in the West African Europhone Novel.* Amsterdam: Rodopi, 1991.

Appendix

Peter Wuteh Vakunta, Ph.D.
le 19 janvier 2011

Professor of Modern Languages
Defense Language Institute

Presidio of Monterey-California

United States of America

Cher M. Ageneau,

J'espère que vous allez très bien. Je suis en communication avec Mme Mercédès Fouda, auteure du roman *Je parle camerounais: pour un renouveau francofaune* que j'ai envie de traduire en anglais pour une plus large diffusion ici aux Etats Unis. Mme Fouda m'a passé vos coordonnées et m'a demandé de vous contacter pour que nous puissions nous entretenir sur la démarche à suivre. Je n'ai pas encore choisi une maison de publication ici en Amérique mais il y en a beaucoup qui vont certainement être interessées par mon projet. Je suis moi-même publié à plusieurs reprises et pourrais me servir d'une maison de publication qui a publié mes livres pour publier la traduction du livre de Mme Fouda, un petit bouquin qui a suscité pas mal d'intérêt ici en Amérique du nord. Veuillez donc, me signaler ce qu'il faudrait faire pour obtenir une permission de traduction de la part de Karthala. Je suis sur Skype et répond au nom de 'vakunta'; ça veut dire que nous pourrions nous entretenir en nous servant de cette voie communicative gratuitement si vous êtes vous-même sur Skype et le préférez ainsi. Dans l'attente de votre réponse, je vous souhaite une journée très agréable.

Cordialement,

Peter W. Vakunta

Editions Karthala
le 23 mai 2011
22-24, Boulevard Arago
75013 Paris, France

Cher monsieur Vakunta,

Avec un grand retard dont je m'excuse, c'est bien volontiers que je vous donne l'autorisation de traduire le livre de Mercédès Fouda: *Je parle camerounais: pour un renouveau francofaune*, qui a été publié aux éditions Karthala en 2001. Je reste à votre disposition pour toutes autres précisions que vous souhaiteriez.

Avec mes salutations les meilleures.

Robert Ageneau,

Directeur des éditions Karthala.

Glossary/Glossaire

A

Abakwa: Bamenda; headquarters of the Northwest Region of Cameroon

Aboki : friend, soya vendor

Achomo: cake

Achouka or ashuka: deserved punishment

Achouka ngongoli: deserved punishment

Aff: affair/ business/ stuff

Akwara: prostitute

Ala: other

Alamibou: magician/ exorcist/ seer

Allô: lie

Ami-ami: friend

A mort: so much

Anaconda: posh car

Ancien: name for someone the speaker does not know

Anglo : anglophone in Cameroon.

Anglofou: pejorative name for Anglophone in Cameroon

Annaba: waterloo of the Indomitable Lions

Anuscratie: homosexuality

Aprem: afternoon

Apprenti-sorcier: opposant

Appuyer: have sexual intercourse with

Arki: locally distilled liquor

Arroser: offer drinks to one's friends

Ashawo: prostitute

Assia (ashia): expression of sympathy

Asso: customer

Atangana bread: bobolo

Attaquant: taxi driver assistant

Attaque: front row of seats in a classroom
Attraper quelqu'un le pilon dans le mortier: catch someone red-handed
Au day: today
Awuf: free of charge
Axe lourd: young prostitute

B

Baba Toura: Ahmadou Ahidjo; president of Cameroon from 1960-1982.
Babtou: a white person/European
Back-back: unlawful dealings
Badluck: misfortune
Bagnole: car
Bahat: ill feelings
Bakassi: any dangerous place
Baleine: state official who embezzles public funds
Bami: short for Bamileke
Banga: pot/ hemp, mariyuana
Bangala: penis
Banquer: to ditch one's partner
Bao: a rich man
Baptiser: steal by sneaking away with money for a service
Barlok: misfortune
Bateau: market
Baton: sum of one million Francs
Bayam sellam: retail tradesman or tradeswoman
Bazo: brand of expensive shoes
Beaucoup beaucoup: in great quantity
Beau-regard: pork or pig
Bebela! gosh!
Bele: unwanted pregnancy
Bendskin: motocyle used for pubic transportation

Bendskinneur: driver of a bendskin
Bep-bep: stammerer/ bragging
Beret-kaki: policeman
Beta: better; I'd rather
Better: would rather/ would better
Beurre: girl's lips
Bibliser: ape the speech of white folks
Biblos: while man/European
Bic: male sexual organs
Bifaka: dried herring
Big bro: elder brother
Big katika: high-ranking official/President of the Republic
Big mater: grandmother
Big pater: grandfather
Big reme: grandmother
Big repe: grandfather
Big rese: elder sister
Bindi: young/ younger/junior
Bindiment: slowly/ gently/softly
Bisness: business
Bita kola: bitter kola
Bled: house, country, village
Blem: problem
Bobi: breast/nipple
Bobi-tenap: brassiere
Bobolo: ground cassava
Bok: prostitute
Bolè: finish/end/ run out of
Bolo: job/work
Boma: boa/rich man who flirts with young girls
Bombo: namesake
Bon-blanc: albino
Bonga: dry fish

Boogie: party/night club
Book: gamble with cards
Bordelle: prostitute
Bordellerie: prostitution
Born: to have a baby
Bosco: bouncer
Boss: boss, manger
Bouffer: refuse to pay back money one has borrowed
Bouffeur: glutton
Bro: short for brother
Boule-zero: close-cut hair
Boum: party
Brancher: to dress well
Branché: well-dressed
Break: break, pause, holiday
Brique: sum of one million francs
Bringue: a party
Bro: short brother
Buche: reading
Buga: dry fish
Bugna: car
Bundja: to score
Bumbu: vagina
Buy: to shop, buy
Buyam-sellam: retailer of food crops
Bye: farewell

C

Ca-aa! interjection expressing surprise
Cacao: young beautiful girl
Cadavéré: dead/ failed project
Cadeau: for free
Café: serious beating

Caillou: something difficult/hard/strenuous

Calculer: to be on the look out for

Calé: pant

Calé-calé: sex between homosexuals

Calékoum: underwear

Callbox: place where a public phone is available, callbox business

Callboxeur: man who does callbox business

Callboxeuse: woman who does callbox business

Calmas: cool down!

Camanglophone: speaker of camfranglais

Camer: Cameroon

Camerien: Camerian, Cameroonian

Camp: indoors/ house/room

Canapé écrasiatique: sofa for love-making

Capo: big shot/mogul/ rich man/friend

Capote: condom

Carreau: match, level

Carry le mbele: become pregnant

Cartouche: lecture notes

Cassé: tired/worn out

C'est how? hello! how is it?

Cha: catch someone

Chain: broke

Chaka: shoes

Cham: room

Chambul: room

Champi: champagne

Champicoter: drink champagne

Changement: change

Chango: address term for men whose wives come from the same family

Chantier: public place or restaurant where food and drinks are sold
Chaud: lover/boyfriend
Chaud gars: hot guy/ Paul Biya/ flirt
Chauffer: to have a sexually transmitted disease
Chavoum: gun
Check: think
Chef: chief/uniformed State official/ police/soldier
Chef-ban: gang leader
Chem: shirt
Chercher: to look for
Chercher la nga d'autrui: court a married woman
Chia: chair/post
Chiba: live or reside in a place
Chichard: niggardly or mean person
Chier: to defecate
Choko: bribe/tip
Chomencam: unemployment in Cameroon
Chop: eat
Chopale: sexually transmitted disease
Chop-broke-pot: selfish person
Chop-bluk-pot: selfish person
Chop chia: heir/successor
Chopper: to contract an STD
Christine: economic crisis
Chuker: kick start a car/ have sex
Chuki: trap
Cinema njoh: a free scene
Cinosh: cinema
Circuit: public place or restaurant where food and drinks are sold
Civiliser: lecture someone
Clando: private car illegally used as a taxi

Class: first-class
Clim: air-conditioner
Close: clothes/ make love
Close les eyes: to persevere/ go ahead/igore a difficulty
Coca-alhadji: insult to Muslims who use coke to color alcoholic drinks
Co-chambrier: room-mate
Coco: girlfriend
Coder: prevent people from seeing something
Coller-chewing gum: very tight/ to gum like chewing gum
Coller-coller: dance tune
Coma: cinema
Comb: have sex/make love
Combi: friend
Come-no- go: disease that causes body to itch
Comment? How are you?
Comot: leave/get out/go out
Comot le corrigé de: produce the best example of
Complice: accomplice/friend
Composer: dupe someone
Condol: condolences
Consti: constipated
Copo: friend
Cops: friend
Coraniser: to cram and recite lecture notes
Corrigé: master copy
Corriger: to make love
Cosh: insult/abuse
Cota: friend/male or female partner
Coupé-décalé: type of music from Côte d'Ivoire
Couper: make love
Cou-plié: rich man
Crâner: to show off; to brag

Crayon: penis
Criquer: to threaten someone
Crish: crazy/drunk/berserk
Cut: extort money from people
Cyclis: tights worn as underwear by women

D

Damba: football
Damer: cooked food/to eat food
Damé: cooked food/to eat food
Dangwa: stroll/walk
Day: there is/day
Dash: faire cadeau/ donner
Débat: woman with a broad waist/with big buttocks
Débré: to try/ to somehow manage
Décapsuler: to deflower a girl
Décapsulage: deflowering a girl
De from: since/ever since
Dégager: remove/get rid of
Dégombotiser: fight against corruption
Dem: give up/abandon/ fail/disappoint
Deme: mess/trouble
Démarrage: state of being sexually aroused
Démarrer: to sexually arouse someone
Den: identity card
Depe: homosexual
Déposer: to leave someone alone
Dépose-moi! leave me alone!
Deps: homosexual
Depso: homosexual
Depuis depuis: a very long time ago
Depuis from: since/ever since/ for a very long time
Deuxième bureau: concubine/illegal sex partner

Diabe: diabetic person
Die: suffer/fail
Diva: to ramble/wander/tell stories
Djigi-djaga: noise and cuddling made by people making love
Djim: big/large
Djim-djim: very big/very large
Djimtété: important person/ mogul/rich person
Djingue: clothes
Djo: friend/partner/man/boy
Djoka: dance/idleness/leisure
Djomba: illegal sex partner/ girlfriend
Djoum: jump
Djoun : drunk; drunkenness
Djuksa: unattractive/horrible
Doc: medical doctor/herbalist
Docta: medical doctor/herbalist
Do: to do/to make
Do: money/dough
Do le hon-hon-hon: to brag/show off/tell lies to win favors
Do le java: to the waltz
Do le mapan: to make love
Do le way: make love
Do moh: to enjoy
Dong pipo: wretch of the earth/underpriviledged
Do two weeks: to spend two weeks
Doser: to measure out something in the right proportions
Doser quelqu'un: to hit someone repeatedly in a fight
Dossier: girl one intends to chat up
Doucement doucement: very slowly or very gently
Doul: Douala
Dribbler: to play truant
DSK: Dominique Strauss-Kahn
Dur: in a hard way

Dybo: someone/a man/important person

E
Eat: to eat
Eat le do: squander money
Eateur: glutton
Eclater: to enjoy oneself
Ecorce: talisman; fetish
Ecraser: make love with a woman
Ecrasage: love-making
Ecraseur: love-maker
Ecrasiatique: for love-making
Ekié! gosh! Interjection expressing surprise
Elobi: swamp
Engin: male or female sex organ
En haut: to be up or appointed
Erreur: mistake/mishap
Etre: to be
Etre en haut: appointed to a post where one can embezzle State funds
Etre frais: to be in good shape
Etre in: to be sexy/to be fashionable
Etre chaud dans quelqu'un: to be broke
Evou: witchcraft
Evu: witchcraft

F
Fafio: money/fortune
Faire ça dur à quelqu'un: to handle someone roughly
Faire comme ça: farewell expression
Fire le mapan: to make love
Fais quoi, fais quoi: No matter what happens/no matter what you think.

Faire: make love/ have sex

Faire chier: injection synonymous with gosh!

Faire le hon-hon-hon: to brag/show off/tell lies to win favors

Faire le java: to the waltz

Falla: search for/have the intention of chatting up a girl

Famla: witchcraft/ sorcery/ fetishism

Fan: to look for

Fan la nga d'autrui: court someone else's girlfriend/wife

Farotter: give out gifts in cash

Farotteur: Saint Nick/ Santa Claus

Faux: false/fake

Faux pass: forged passport

Feel: to feel/have feelings

Fesser: to have sexual intercourse

Feu (être le feu): to be difficult

Fey: to scam/to dupe/fool/deceive/swindle somebody

Feyman: con man; scammer

Feymania: trickery/swindling

Feywoman: con woman

Fictionner: make love/have sex

Fiesta: party

Fifty-fifty: equal sharing

Fika: to have sexual intercourse

Fmisé: to be hit by economic crisis

Finir: drink too much/be exhausted

Finir avec quelqu'un : to achieve one's goal

Fire: risk/ danger/failure/ fire/trouble/emergency

Flash: dry cough

Flop: many/complete/numerous

Flo: cigarette

Foi: short for foirage

Foirage: state of being broke/poverty/hardship

Foirer: to be broke

Fok: make love
Folon: vegetable dish
Fom: to have sexual intercourse
Foup-foup: disorder
Fraicheur: young beautiful woman
Frais: in good shape/ financially sound/ elegant
Francho: frankly
Frangin: village dweller/friend/someone living in the rural area
Frappe: dupery
Frappeur: conman
Fringueur: someone who dresses well
Frog: francophone Cameroonian
Front: reading
Fronter: to read for long/ to study hard
Fuck: copulate/make love

G
Galère: hardship
Galérer: to be facing hard times
Gandura: gown
Garder: to take along a gift
Garer: to stand someone up
Gari: a bribe
Gars: friend/boyfriend
Gata: prison
Gengerou: albino
Gengeru: albino
Gee: give
Gérant: someone who goes out with a girl
Gérer: to go out with a girl
Ghettosard: someone who lives in a poverty-stricken area
Gib: give
Gif: give

Ginger: something difficult to do

Gio: to play

Gip: give

Gnama: food/to eat

Gneps: type of cake

Gnole: car, especially a luxury one

Godasse: social connections

Gombo: bribe/tip/money/ financial benefits

Gombiste: one who is highly motivated by financial gain

Gombotique: related to corruption

Gombotiser: to give a bribe

Gomme: a type of slippers made out of rubber

Gomna: government/governor/ police officer// manager

Gonfler: to brag/boast

Graf-fo-de: piss off/get lost/to go hell

Grafi: people from the grassfields of Cameroon

Grand: elder brother, form of address

Grand brother: elder brother

Grand Camarade: El Hajj Ahmadou Ahidjo

Grattage: flattering

Gratter: to flatter someone

Grave: very much/too much

Grillé: someone who has nothing to lose

Grimba: witchcraft

Grimbatique: related to witcraft

Grimbatiser: protect property with fetish

Gué: cannabis

Gui: girl

Guitare: type of skin disease

H

Haa: strong home-made liquor

Hala: to hassle/scold/scream

Haba! interjection of surprise

Half-book: illiterate

Hambok: to worry or disturb

Hap: nothing

Haricot: female genitalia

Haut: up/ high-ranking

Hear: listen/obey

Helele: interjection of surprise/wonderful thing

Helep: help

Hia: hear/listen/obey

Hier-hier: novice

High: on drugs

Hiish! interjection expressing a feeling of repugnance

Hoha: attitude similar to that of a bully

Homme- Lion: Lion Man/ Paul Biya/President of Camreroon

Hon-hon-hon: bragging/nonsensical talk

Hon-hon: to brag

Hop-eye: bullying/ using force to make someone do something

Hosto: hospital

Hot: difficult/busy/tease someone

Hot la tête: make someone think

How? : Hi

How-no? What really?

How que? How come?

Hyper: excessive

Hyper hot: very busy

I
ID: identity card

If: if

Il y a match: the stakes are high

Imbook: illiterate

In: in vogue
Intello: intellectual/Learned person

J

Jach*è*re: period of loneliness for a girl/ long period without having sex
Jaf: food/to eat
Jaka: boyfriend/partner
Jambo: gambling
Jamboteur: gambler
Jamboula: night club
Janga: small/slim/slender/little
Jazz: cooked beans
Jazz sous-marin: beans submerged in cooking oil
Jazzer: to eat beans
Jazzeur: someone who eats beans regularly
Jeune talent: Jeune homme, jeune fille,
Je wanda: I wonder
Jembe: to reach climax during sexual intercourse
Jetons: coins/change
Jia: listen/obey
Jim: very big
Jo: guy/boy
Jobajo: locally brewed beer
Johnny: to pad/tramp/walk/ to walk a long distance
Johnny-Four-Foot: goat/idiot
Joka: a party
Jomba: illegal sex partner/ girlfriend
Jong: drink alchohol
Jongeur: drunkard
Jong man: drunkard
Jos: judge, discuss, argue
Juju-kalabar: monster/something frightful

Jus: judge, discuss, argue

K

Kaba: gown worn by pregnant women

Kaba nyango: large gown worn by women

Kai! Expression of anger/surprise

Kamambrou: soldier

Kako: girl one is courting

Kamer: Cameroon/truncation of Kamerun

Kamerlock: Cameroonian doldrums

K-merlock: Cameroonian doldrums

Kam-no- go: disease that causes one's body to itch

Kanda: testicles/cowhide/ belt

Kan-kan: several/something difficult

Kanda: belt/cowhide

Kapo: mogul/ rich person/ friend

Kassa: term used for northerners in Cameroon

Katakata: cunning/good at deceiving

Katika: God/ boss/director/ person who manages a betting business or movie hall

Keep: to keep

Keep quelqu'un: to take along a gift

Kef: tired/exhausted

Keleng keleng: a local type of spinach

Kenekene: okra/slippery/ a local type of spinach

Kengue: Imbecile/idiot/foolish person

Kenzo: brain of expensive shoes

Kerenkeren: okra/slippery/ a local type of spinach

Keulan: aim/target

Ketouh: policeman/ gendarme

Kick: steal/rob

Kicker: rob/steal

Kickman: thief

Kickwoman: thief

Kilombo: person who gets paid to take an exam for somone else

Kin: steal/rob

Knack kanda: have sex

Know: master/ be aware of something

Koki: meal of beans cake

Kolo: 1000 francs CFA/ a thousand

Kolo-fap: 1500 francs CFA

Komot: come out/ go out

Kombi: friend/young man

Kombo: have sexual intercourse

Kondre: nation/country

Kondre talk; vernacular language/mother tongue

Kong: witchcraft

Kongolibon: close-cropped

Kongossa: gossip/back-biting

Kop niè: to watch out/ to be careful

Koppo: friend/boyfriend/close friend

Kosam: yahout

Kosh: insult

Koss-koss: high-heel shoes

Kossovo: poor neighborhood near a rich neighborhood

Kota: friend/ female or male partner

K.O: Knock out

Kotto: a crippled person

Koukouma: high-ranking officer/ President of the Republic

Krenkren: okra/slippery/ a local type of spinach

Krish: mad/crazy

Kumba: counterfeit birth certificate

Kumbu: big dish/ soup tureen

Kunia-kunia: slowly/gently

Kung-fu: crafty strategy

Kwa: bag, especially a small one
Kwat: neighborhood/ district in a city
Kwata: neighborhood/ district in a city
Kwem: meal of cassava leaves
Kwench: to die

L
Laf: laugh
Lage: village
Lai: to tell a lie
Lancer: to head for
Lancer quelqu'un: to give someone money/to praise someone
Lang: to read
Langa: mouth watering
Lass: buttocks
Langua: speak/tell/talk
Lap: laugh
Lapant: funny/ridiculous
Las: occurring /taking place after hours
Lass: buttocks/private parts
Lassa: stupid person
Lass man: stupid person
Lep: leave
L'eau: leaked examination questions
L'homme Lion:/Lion Man/ Paul Biya
Libérer: agree to make love
Lob: to smoke marijuana
Lob man: drug addict
Loko: to brag
Lolos: breasts, especially very large ones
Lom: to tell lies
Londo: to brag
Long: house/home/residence/room

Long crayon: literate folks/ educated people/intellectuals
Longo-longo: talla and slim
Lookot fire: rubber shoes
Loss: die/misplace
Loss sense: fool
Lookot: watch out
Lourd: financially buoyant
Lys: short for lycee

M

Ma: to think up
Maboya: whore
Macabo: grudge
Macro: crook
Madiba: leaked exam questions
Mafio: criminal
Mafioso: mafia/dealer/swindler
Magan: witchcraft
Magni: mother of twins
Maguida: Muslim from northern Cameroon
Mainant: now
Malamb: bait
Makalapati: bribe/tip
Makandi: vagina
Make le java: to do the waltz
Mamba: ten thousand francs
Ma mami! Gosh!
Mamie: elderly woman, business woman of a certain age
Mami-pima: mother's vagina
Mami-nyanga: good looking lady
Mami-wata: female water spirit
Man Bassa: male person of Bassa origin
Mange-mille: corrupt police-officer

Management: items of corruption
Mangues: breasts
Manières: childish behavior
Manif: manifestation
Maquis: cruel of wicked person/ member of the underground military wing of the Cameroon People's Union in the late 1960's
Mara: marathon
Manioc: vagin/ genitals of a woman
Ma own: mine/my own
Marabout: undesirable person
Massa: Sir/ Mister/friend/ term of surprise
Masho: term of address for mother
Matanga: type of rubber shoes
Matango: palm wine
Match: sexual intercourse
Mater: mother
Matin, midi, soir: all the time/ all day
Max: maximum
Maxi: maximum
Maux de poche: shortage of resources/ being broke
Mazembe: bandit
Mbambe: menial job
Mbele: pregnancy
Mbeng: Europe
Mbengue: Europe
Mbenguiste: someone who travels to Europe
Mbengueter: travel regularly abroad
Mbere-Khaki: policeman
Mbeuh! What a pity!
Mbindi: small/junior/young/young person
Mbit: penis/male genitalia
Mboa:home country/Cameroon

Mbock: prostitute

Mboko: outside world

Mbom: young man

Mbombo: homonym/namesake/friend

Mbomtolo: fat

Mbourou: money

Mbout: idiot/fool

Mboutoucou: idiot/fool

Mboutman: idiot/fool

Mbra: term of address

Mbut: idiot/ foolish person/coward

Meder: Mercedez car

Megan: witchcraft/fetish

Mémé: young beautiful girl

Même-même: precisely

Même père, même mère: nuclear siblings

Meng: die/kill

Merco: Mercedes car/luxury car

Merco, gombo, dodo: hustle and bustle of city life.

Metosh: half- breed/light-skinned person

Mettre quelqu'un en haut: appoint someone to a high position

Meuf: young girl one desires/girl-friend

Mifa: family

Milito: soldier

Mimba: bragging/showing off

Mimbayance; bragging/showing off

Mimbo: liquor/ alcoholic drink

Mimboland: Cameroon

Mingri: slender/slim/skinny

Minion: appetite

Mini minor: woman of small build

Mof-me-de: piss off

Moh: very good/satisfactory

Mola: man/fellow
Molo: gently
Molo-molo: very gently/slowly
Mome: young girl/woman in general
Money-man: rich person
Mon type: man/ someone whose name is forgotten
Mop: mouth
Moronto: confuse or trick someone
Mortier: female sexual organ/vagina
Motivation: bribe/tip
Mougou: fool/idiot
Mouiller: sexually arouse
Moumie: young beautiful girl one desires
Mouser: to brag
Moussong: mystical illness which makes the body rot
Moumou: weak person/coward
Mouv: partying
Mov me dey: an expression of surprise or admiration
Moyen: financial resources
Moyo: form of address/financial means
Mpoti: having group sex
Mua: add/raise
Mukala: albino/mulatto
Mukuanye: cult
Mukwaye: witchcraft/fetish
Mulongo: whip
Mumu: deaf and dumb/stupid person/coward
Mutmut: gnat
Muna: kid/girlfriend/baby
N
Na: is; it is
Na how? hello! how is it?
Nack: to tell

Nack les divers: chat/gossip

Nak: beat/defeat

Na lie!: It's not true!

Nang: sleep/spend the night

Nanga-boko: dirty, filty person

Nassara: white person

Nayor: slowly

Nayor-nayor: very slowly/ very gently

Nchinda: page/servant

Ndamba: football match

Ndeme: mess/trouble

Ndiba: water

Ndolo: love

Ndole: national vegetable dish

Ndoleiser: to eat a dish of ndole

Ndombolo: fat/stout woman/fat buttocks

Ndomo: fight

Ndopa: cigarette/tobacco

Ndos: smart person

Ndou:money

Ndoutou: ill-luck/bad luck

Ndutu: ill-luck/bad luck

Negos: negotiation

Ness: business

Nga: girl/female partner

Ngata: prison

Ngataman: prisoner

Ngi: female partner/girl

Ngo: girl

Ngo: short for Ongola

Ngola: Cameroon

Ngomna: government

Ngondele: young girl

119

Ngueme: poverty
Ngum: strength/power
Ngui: female partner/girl
Niama niama: small/ of little value/worthless/useless person
Nian: sell one's personal belongings
Nian-nian: brand new
Niang! : expression of defiance
Nianga: stylish/well-dressed
Nie: see
Nindja: police man/soldier
Nioxer: fuck, screw, have sexual relations with someone
Njoh: free of charge
Njoka: a party
Njoter: free of charge
Njoteur: opportunist
Nkane: prostitute
Nkap: money/fortune/resources
Nkui: meal of brownish color
Noyaux: testicles
Now now so: right now/right away
Ntamulung choir: useless noise/brouhaha
Ntong: luck/opportunity
Nucer: suck a girl's lips/kiss a girl passionately
Nyama nyama: very small/ of little significance or value
Nye: see
Nyoxer: fuck, screw, have sexual relations with someone
Numéro six: intelligence/perspicacity

O

Obosoh! gosh!
O'day: today
Odontol: locally distilled liquor
Oiseau: chicken, bird

Okrika: second-hand clothes

On fait comme ça: Ok, see you later!

Oncal: uncle

One-man-show: bragging/boasting

Ongola: Cameroon/Yaounde

Ongolais: Cameroonian

On vous connaît! We know how dishonest you are!

Opep: private car used illegally for transporting passengers

Opposant: member of an opposition party

Ordi: computer

Organe de base: male genital organs

Over: too much

Oya: oil/grease

P

Pacho: father

Pa Pol: Paul Biya

Padre: Prêtre

Paff: corn pap

Palava: affaire

Pample-porc: grapefruit and pork

Paplé: surprised/unbelievable/unthinkable/mad

Parler: give a bribe/corrupt a public official

Pass: passport

Pater: father

Pays-bas: genital organs

Pederastie: gay practices

Penia: new

Penya penya: very new/ in very good state

Pep: leave/go away

Pepe: girlfriend

Pepper: hot/difficult

Perfusion: drip

Perika: Petit frère
Petite: girlfriend
Piak: to sneak away
Piaule: residence/apartment
Pif: fall in love
Pilon: male sexual organ/penis
Piol: residence/apartment
Piole: residence/apartment
Pipo: people
Pistachage: love-making
Pistache: female genital organ/vagina
Pistacheur: love-maker
Pistachique: related to love-making
Plantain: male genital organ/penis
Pointage: paid menial job
Pointer: do a paid menial job
Politiquart: politician
Popaul: Paul Biya/ nick-name for the President of Cameroon
Pote: mate/friend
Potopoto: mud/low-cost house built with mud
Pousseur: truck pusher
Poum: sneak away
Pratiquer: practice occult rituals
Prendre quelqu'un le pilon dans le mortier: catch someone red-handed
Preso: condom
Pression: pressure
Pro: problem/professional
Probat: secondary school certificate

Q
Quat: neighborhood/ quarter/residential area
Quata: neighborhood/ quarter/ residential area

Quartier: neighborhood/ quarter/ residential area
Quota: male or female partner/friend

R

Radio trottoir: rumor
Rangers: type of strong canvas shoes
Raser: disgrace someone
Rationner: provide money for food
Reach: arrive/reach
Reback: return/ come back/go back/resume
Recame: return/ come back/go back/resume
Rdépéciste: member of the CPDM in Cameroon/member of the ruling party
Refre: brother
Rego: return/ come back/go back
Reme: mother
Renault-deux: walk/tramp/trek
Repe: father
Rese: sister
Ricain/recaine: American
Roi-Faineant: Lazy king; lame duck president
Rond: money
Rythmner: go out with a girl but not make love with her
Rythmeur: someone who goes out with a girl but does not make love with her

S

Sabitout: know-all
Sabi: know
Saccager; make love exhaustively
Saka: dance/go to a nightclub
Salaka: sacrifice
Samara: sandals made of cow hide

Sango: man/sir
Sansanboy: smart boy/young lad
Sans-con: rubber-made slippers
Sans-payer: a police-van
Sapak: whore
Sapeur: someone who dresses well
Saper: dress well
Sara: white man/woman
Saraka: sacrifice
Sauveteur: hawker; peddler
Science: think/ponder
Secteur: spot where hawkers sell their goods
Sentir quelqu'un: feel someone's ruthlessness/power
Se sucrer: to embezzle public funds
Seven plus one: AIDS
Sexy: see through outfit
Shaba: war-torn/poverty-stricken
Shake: to dance
Shap: early morning
Shap shap: very early in the morning
Sherif: rich man
Shiba: live/reside in a place
Show le pepper: to trouble/disturb
Siba: live/reside in a place
Silencieux: 100 CFA francs
Sissia: intimidate someone
Sista: sister
Sita: sister
Sitak: taxi
Situass: occasion/event
Small: minor
Small no be sick: popular Chinese balm
Sortir le corrigé de: produce the best example of

Sotuc: prostitute
Soya: roasted meat sold near pubs
Sous-quat: ghetto/slum
Souteneur: boyfriend or husband
States: USA
Stationnement: parking
Statois: someone who has been to the USA
Story: gossip
String: type of female dress
Sucre: girlfriend
Swa: fear
Swit-mimbo: pop/soda
Swine: abuse term
Swolo: swallow
Squatter: to live/stay

T

Taco: taxi
Tanap: stand up
Tara: accomplice
Taff: cigarette
Tagne: father of twins
Tailler: run away
Tai-toi: bribe
Takesh: taxi
Tango: soft beverage obtained by adding some syrup to beer
Tanner: make love exhaustively
Tantal: aunt/any sister or half-sister
Tantine: aunt
Tara: friend
Tarcler: foul play in soccer
Taxi-opep: private car used illegally for transporting passengers
Tcha: catch someone red-handed

Tcha quelqu'un le pilon dans le mortier: catch someone red-handed

Tchango: address term for men whose wives come from the same family

Tchat: chat up a girl

Tchatcher: chat up a girl

Tchatcheur: some who knows how to enterain women

Tchoko: tip/bribe

Tchotchoro: small/not mature

Tchouquer: jump start a car/make love

Tchouqueur: womanizer

Tchouki: domain under one's control

Teboi: nightclub

Tell: recount/ tell/alert/inform

Tempo: watch out!

Tensionner: anger/bother

Terma: mother

Terminer: make love exhaustively

Terpa: father

Testo: testicles

Tété: important person/rich man

Tif: thief/steal

Timor: bully

Timoriser: to bully/frighten

Titi: girl

Titulaire: preferred girlfriend

Titus: preferred girlfriend

Tobassi: charm/spell/mystical power

Tok: talk/speak

Tokio: run away

Toli: gossip/story

Tong: luck/opportunism

Tonner: to abuse/insult

Tonton: uncle/respectable person
Ton-ton: keep on giving fake appointments
Top: first class/nice
Topo: story/talk
Tori: gossip/story
Tosh: begging for a stick of cigarette
Tosher: beg for a stick of cigarette
Toshme: half-breed
Toto: incompetent person
Touch: to touch

Toum: sell one's personal belonging
Tourne-dos: turn-back restaurant/ makeshift restaurant, roadside restaurant where cheap food is sold
Tracer: go away
Trois V (travail, villa, virement): car, house, bank transfer.
Troisième pied: penis
Trong: difficult
Tsuip: sign of disrespect
Truanteur: thief
Tuber: tuberculosis
Tuer: to have sex with a woman
Tuyau: bribe channel/nightclub
Tuyauriste: party-goer
Type: man whose name the speaker doesn't know/way of addressing an unknown person
U
Understand: to understand
Up: short for up-eye/bullying

V
Valise: one's best clothes
Vaps: attraction to someone

Vass: to wash
Vendre: to sell
Vendre quelqu'un au famla: bewitch someone
Vendre quelqu'un au kong: bewitch someone
Vendre quelqu'un au nyiongo: bewitch someone
Ventre: witcraft/stomach
Verber: talk/chat
Vere: dream
Vernis haoussa: Hausa vanish
Vesté: wearing a suit
Viens-on-reste: living together but not married
Vieux: father/parents
Villakonkon: uncivilized person/rustic
Villaps: uncivilized persons/rustics/ ill-mannered person
Voisin: neighbor whose name one does not know
Voiso: neighbor
Voum: bragging
Vrai-de-dieu! : By God!
Vrai-vrai: truly

W

Wanda: wonder/be surprised
Wadjax: Muslim from one of the three northern regions of Cameroon
Wadjo: Muslim from one of the three northern regions of Cameroon
Wah: woman or girl one desires
Wai: address term for someone from the northern part of Cameroon
Waka: walk/stroll/function/girl searching for a husband
Walai! interjection expressing anger
Wangala (variant of bangala): male genital organ
Wash: take a bath

Way: means/money
Wekop: to wake up
Whitiser: to speak with a European accent
Win:to win
Wise: smart
White: European
Win: succeed
Wok: work/job
Wolowoss: prostitute/loose-living girl
Wowo: bad/not attractive

Y
Ya: hear/listen/understand
Ya: your
Ya moh: enjoy/be satisfied
Ya bad: suffer
Yam: yam
Yam-fufu: pounded fresh yam eaten with soup
Yamo: to like someone or something
Yelo pepe: type of pepper
Yemale! : Gosh!
Yong: to regret
Yesso: said to signify approval
Yeush: expression of disgust
Yich: interjection of disgust
Yotass: money
Youa: your
Yua: your
Yus: use
Yusles: useless
Yuropian: whiteman/European
Yut: youth
Yi: his/her/its

Yi on: his/her/its own
Yo: young boy that dresses up well
Yoh: young boy that dresses up well
Yoyette: young girl that dresses up well

Z

Zamba: God
Zamzam: very big/very large
Zangalewa: soldier
Zapper: ditch a lover/break up or end a relationship
Zeke-zeke: sex
Zen: able to keep one's composure
Zhon: drunk
Zik: short for music
Zikmu: short for music
Zinc: any card of diamond suit
Zingué: popular danse close to makossa
Zion: to be high on drugs or alcohol
Ziro: zero
Zoroh: allowing the ball to pass between one's legs in a game of soccer
Zouazoua: fuel of doubtful origin/ illicit fuel sold clandestinely in Cameroon
Zoze: male genitalia/penis
Zuazua: fuel of doubtful origin/ illicit fuel sold clandestinely in Cameroon

Index

Beignet 14
Beignetariat 14
Bendskin 48
Benskinneur 48
Berman 67
Beti 19
Beti language 19
Big Katika 51, 55
Binarism 84
Bloom 85
Bloom's Taxonomy 85
Bloominan taxonomy 85
Bloomian Taxonomic Model 85
Bobolo 17
Borrowing 1
Buber 86
Buea 44, 50, 52

C

Calque 4, 13, 66, 70
Camer 44, 78
Camerian 50, 54, 63
Camerian Anthem 54, 63
Camerien 43
Cameroon 1, 10, 46, 47, 65
Cameroonian 2, 23, 75
Cameroonianism 24
Cameroonization 18
Cameroun 44, 46
Camerounisme 3, 68, 70
Camfranglais 1, 2, 3, 4, 5, 6, 7, 8, 9, 10, 12, 14, 17, 21, 27, 31, 65, 75, 76, 79
Camfranglais literature 24, 27, 83, 84
Camfranglophone 7, 20, 25, 69, 79
Camfranglais discourse 17
Camfranglophone discourse 25
Camp Sic 43, 50
Carole de Feral 2
Cassava 17, 76
Catford 75

132

Chairman 59, 62, 78, 80, 81
Choko 52
Chop 3
Chop Pipo Dem Moni Party 48
Chomencam 46, 48, 73
Clando 25
Clipping 9
Code 1, 13, 71
Code alternation 9
Code –mixing 2, 7, 9, 15, 25, 71
Code-switching 1, 9, 16, 20,
Coffee 53
Colonization 11
Come-no-go 62
Composite language 1
Compound 77
Compounding 25
Constipated constitution 55
Creole 75
Crocodile 40
Cultural dynamism 16
Cultural relativity 24
Cultural specificity 23
Cultural semantics 77

D
Damba 3
Damer 3
Debe 3
Dem 44
Discourse 10, 14, 17, 22
Djimtete 57
Djo 10
Docta Lesigha 62
Domestication 75, 77
Domestication of French 75
Douala 58
Duala 71

Jones 13, 66, 74

Sukulu 4

Y

Yaounde 3, 58, 76
Yo 23
Yoyette 23

Z

Zabus 7, 11
Zangalewa 44, 52, 61
Zang Zang 2
Zero 40
Zouazoua 76, 77